# Leading Self

Leading for Social Responsibility and Sustainable Development

## Stig Zandrén

**Front page:**
Montreal, Canada - April 22, 2012: People manifesting and walking for
Jour de la Terre (Earth Day) in the streets of Montreal,
Source: iStock by Getty Images

**Original title:**
Ledning sökes – Om ledarskap för
socialt ansvarstagande och hållbarhet, 2012

**Publisher:**
BoD – Books on Demand GmbH, Stockholm, Sweden

**Print:**
BoD – Books on Demand GmbH, Norderstedt, Germany

**ISBN:**
978-91-7699-609-6

www.bod.se

# CONTENTS

**AUTHOR & ACKNOWLEDGEMENTS**          5

**COMMENTS** on *Ledning sökes*          7

**PROLOGUE**          9

**PART I:**     **CONTEXT**
Chapter 1:     Leading Self          17
Chapter 2:     The Task          39
Chapter 3:     The Team          57

**PART II:**     **DEVELOPMENT**
Chapter 4:     Awareness          81
Chapter 5:     Dialogue          103
Chapter 6:     Phronesis          129

**EPILOGUE**          147

**APPENDICES**
Appendix 1:     Glossary          153
Appendix 2:     References          165
Appendix 3:     The FIRO Theory          171

# AUTHOR & ACKNOWLEDGEMENTS

## Stig Zandrén

Photo: Gunnar Reinerdahl

I am an Aquarius, born in 1945, more than a decade after my three elder brothers.

My work experience started in the area of strategic planning and investment analysis for the Swedish Defense Research and for Volvo Car. In 1978, I turned into logistics and management consulting. Lars O Södahl was my boss and coach for eight years, the brain behind Asset Management – ways of thinking for raising productivity by more efficient use of capital tied-up.

In the mid 80's, I started on my 'second professional leg' – human functioning, personal and leadership development. I am a qualified user of a number of concepts for personal growth, collaboration and organizational development.

My mentor was Arne Derefeldt, an early adopter of modern human resource approaches like sensitivity training, transactional analysis, mentoring and coaching. Thanks to Arne, I got in touch with William C Schutz (Will), the founder of the FIRO theory and The Human Element. Will trained and certified me as a facilitator of The Human Element.

Lars, Arne and Will have passed away. They are alive in my mind inspiring me to apply, refine and share their ideas.

I am very grateful to Dag Rudqvist, my professional companion for many years in practising and developing Wills ideas as expressed in The Human Element training. Dags interpretation of the FIRO theory in appendix 3 represents our common conclusions.

I also want to acknowledge Hans Lindberg, my editor, who continuously follows and supports my work – especially for correcting and complementing my translation and reworking of my first book, *Ledning sökes,* into this book.

# COMMENTS on *Ledning sökes*

A very readable book and a valuable complement to the field of leadership and leading processes. The book gives objective and scientific illustrations of many aspects of leadership and of co-operation between leaders and collaborators. The main focus is on psychosocial processes and sustainable development. Despite all the facts, the book is easy to read and pedagogical. The book is therefore suitable for courses and studies. At the same time, some sections are as inspiring, motivating and reflecting as a good sermon.

**Anna Rosengren,** *priest and ethics consultant, Etik i arbetslivet AB*

A very well written book in which Stig reflects on his experiences from his full professional life. He pays attention to Stephen Covey, Will Schutz and others. Stig also writes about the challenge of the current society, a society that finds it hard to control and with companies just waiting. We cannot wait and everyone needs to be more aware of their choices.

**Per Larshans,** *(2012) Chief Sustainability Officer, Max Hamburgerrestauranger AB*

People need a completely different type of leadership than those leaders and managers who have created the chaos that prevails in the world in 2012. Stig Zandrén's book *Ledning sökes* shows in a meritorious way that the world needs leaders who think in new ways and how these ways can look like.

**Håkan Lagergren,** *author and designer of the UID Future Map*

*Ledning sökes* is not a book for beginners in organizational psychology. It is a book for those who have read much about the subject and who want to go on with their own thoughts. Stig Zandrén gives many examples of theoretical models which function as a quick course in organizational psychology, a kind of 'psychology for dummies', for us who do not follow the current psychological discussion. And that is good enough.

**Marianne Berg,** *social worker and journalist,*
*the company* Ord & Handling *(Word & Action)*


This personally written and experience based leadership philosophy is well connected anchored in current research. It has a wide theoretical base and mirrors an optimistic attitude towards the current challenges. The personal address adds another dimension – an invitation to the reader to co-create.

**Bosse Forsén,** *BTJ spring 2012*

# PROLOGUE

This book is inspired by and dedicated to my great mentor, Will Schutz (1924–2002). He was a psychologist and also a scholar who managed to integrate his scientific platform with a wide range of experiential learning. I especially appreciated his ability and drive to demonstrate that human emotions and feelings are essential factors behind what is going on between us and in our organizations. He brought feelings into the open and created a unique pedagogic for training us to be aware of, accept and appreciate our emotional self. In his last book, *The Human Element – Productivity, Self-Esteem and the Bottom Line,* Schutz made these fundamental statements about the connection between self and leadership:

- *At the heart of all human functioning is the self.*

- *Best solutions to organizational and leadership issues require self-awareness as an essential first step.*

- *Deeper self-awareness leads to self-acceptance and then self-esteem.*

- *As individuals gain self-awareness and self-esteem, they become more open and honest with their co-workers. They redirect the energy they now use for defensiveness, withholding, and other interpersonal struggles into productive work.*

After my first professional twenty years as a logistics consultant these statements became a key to my understanding of what is going on in organizations and in myself. I spent another couple of decades as a trainer of The Human Element seminars, applying and refining Will Schutz' ideas, introducing them in different contexts, such as business, schools and peace work.

The purpose of this book is to inspire those of you who work in organizations, as leaders or co-workers, to reflect on your self and your organization, but also on people and organizations around and on human functioning in society. I have chosen to focus on the leading process, the interaction between the leader and the co-worker in groups and in specific contexts. The self and the team are assumed to have the task to improve the conditions for human functioning and community. How can we together, through leading and leadership, create good circumstances for people to face the task – - to improve and develop?

A specific task targeted in the subtitle is enhancing conditions for sustainability as by now expressed in the Sustainable Development Goals (SDG) and in The Paris Agreement, both adopted in 2015. The need for better co-ordinated leading processes on a global level is obvious. How can each of us take responsibility and contribute?

My starting point is the way I think, consciously and unconsciously. Which are my basic assumptions about myself, the conceptual basis for my self-esteem. Are the assumptions formed in my childhood still relevant? Are there other ways of thinking about myself that are more relevant today? What do I think of myself when approaching and being in groups?

Our basic assumptions and self-esteem guide our approaches to the outside world. Our different ways of thinking are inputs to co-operation – and they also seem to quite often create obstacles. At the same time, working together seems to be something we humans are made for. How can we create good circumstances for co-operation? How do we take responsibility for ourselves - for our thoughts, feelings and behaviors?

On the one hand, I believe that we need to rethink in order to go from the last 200 years of extraordinary development to a feasible future for human beings on this planet. Our ways of thinking determine – and also limit – our capacity to meet global challenges in relevant and efficient ways, some of the most urgent being climate change, health conditions and human rights. There is an urgent need for questioning current ways of thinking and opening up for radical rethinking.

On the other hand, I think that everyone has a big unused potential to change mindset and ways of doing things. We all have hereditary, conscious and unconscious perceptions of what is wise to do. In the last 100 years or so, knowledge of human functioning and interpersonal relating has expanded tremendously. This development of the human sciences, I find affecting the public mindsets much less than the equally expanded knowledge of technology and the natural sciences.

This book consists of two major parts: CONTEXT and DEVELOPMENT. The Context part is about the concepts of leading and leadership, task, self and team. In the Development part I share my experience and insight within three phases of a personal development process:

1)  Becoming aware
2)  Relating to new awareness through dialogue with yourself and others
3)  Acting wisely on the basis of new experience and insight.

Acting wisely stands for *reflecting on intentions and consequences related to our actions*. Especially, I want to raise the question of our responsibility for our 'backpack' – traumas, emotional memories, and other earlier experiences which might threaten our self-esteem today. The leader's behavior has impact upon the functioning of as well the organization as the individual co-workers. In an urgent and critical situation the consequences of the leader's hidden trauma combined with low self-esteem can be disastrous. From this point of view, I find it important and self-evident that we all explore our life experiences, enhance our self-awareness, and take responsibility for our self-esteem.

Below is a summary of ideas on leading and leadership to be found in this book. Leading and leadership are two sides of the same coin and self is the common de-nominator – the leader's self and personal leadership, and the self-leadership of other selves being led. As-suming free will means that all of us are free to choose how to act. How can I influence other's choice to act – if at all?

THINK
- be clear about context and the task
- set up your ethical guidelines
- create driving force, for instance through a vision
- explore your self and your organization

RELATE
- know and be yourself
- take responsibility for your self-esteem
- be in the center of the team
- be empathic

INFLUENCE
- engage:    release energy, competence and compassion
- motivate:  stimulate initiative, taking responsibility
             and caring
- act::      be a model, turn and twist, complement
             the team

The ideas and suggestions in this book are not unique.
My intention is to focus on ideas which I have learnt to
appreciate – and invite you to try them out for yourelf.
I do not ask you to be instrumental and strictly follow
some rules. It is when you have made yourself aware of
these and other ideas, reflected on them, tried them
out and made them unconscious, that you can function
intuitively and relevantly as a leader and as a co-
worker.

'Leading self' is applicable to any specific context.
Since many selves normally participate in the leading
process – inside as well as outside the team – it is my
intention to show how each of us can engage in and
contribute to leading these selves. Sometimes it is 'the
last drop' which triggers change and you might be the
one supplying that drop.

# PART I

# CONTEXT

# 1    LEADING SELF

## 1.1    Concepts and Definitions

*Leadership does not reside in a person but in an arena that can be occupied by offerings of specific wisdom to the needs of the community. ...... Leadership for this era is not a role or a set of traits; it's a zone of interrelational process. Step in, step out.*
Nora Bateson

This book is based on the idea that *every human has the potential to contribute to change in the environment that one is a part of.* Be it a local association, a private company, a national parliament or a global network. The personal and inner challenge for each of us is to be enough aware of situations and relate to this awareness in a wise, clever and caring manner. The external challenges, such as population growth and energy supply, bring people together in groups, companies, nation states and global networks. Managing nature and society on planet Earth concerns all human beings and the human species. In the meeting between the inner world of an individual and the external systems, responsibility and leading are two important aspects.

I want to make a distinction between *leading* and *leadership*. Leading is the process in which leadership is exercised. Leadership stands for *the way in which a person leads and influences* while leading stands for *a process and the task to move in a certain direction.* Traditionally, leadership is something personal. Leading is connected to a social system and a management process. Leading can be based on agreements between those committed to the management function and to the assignment of exercising personal leadership.

Much has been written about leadership and management in modern times, especially the last 100 years. The amount of references indicates that there are as many definitions of leadership as there are authors. Lena Lid Andersson made in her thesis from 2009 an overview of the research and the literature. She found close to 15,000 books about leadership up to 2003. Content and underlying research can be differentiated into three different aspects of leadership:

- the leader as a person – profile, behavior and charisma
- contingency in the situation
- leading as a process

Interaction between personal leadership and the social context makes the field of leadership development complex. Henry Mintzberg argues that it is impossible to educate leaders and also to train leaders to act in any organization. The most successful and admired leaders have been trained in the prevailing culture they are to act in. My current examples are IKEA's founder Ingvar Kamprad and the late leader of Apple, Steve Jobs.

The word 'lead' has different connotations and that is one aspect of the conceptual difficulty. To lead means 1) to be first and foremost in relation to others, 2) to be responsible for, and 3) to be the initiator of something. Especially the first meaning is problematic. To place an expert, supervisor or manager outside or above the others in a group is like controlling people by sending signals from outside to their brains.

The management function in an organization can be compared to the central nervous system of a human being and the leading process to the co-ordination between the neurons in the brain. Collaborators contribute to leading by following the formal leaders and also by taking initiatives when the formal leader fails or needs to be completed. There is hierarchy. In case of emergency, the central leadership takes over – in the same way as 'the reptile brain'. In a crisis situation, it is often too late to include the ideas of collaborators – the frontal lobe. However, human brains and organizations can practice confronting imagined events, for instance by training in simulated crisis situations. A successful Swedish skier, Ingemar Stenmark, once said in an interview: "It seems that the more I practice the more luck I have".

An assumption in this book is that all of us in a social system have impact upon each other. Each of us has impact upon the groups we are in. I will argue that we have the ability to become aware of the power we exercise and to choose our actions. How we relate to others is a function of how we relate to ourselves. Accordingly I have a personal responsibility to explore and, when needed, to adapt my behavior to 1) the context, 2) collaborators and other persons involved and 3) myself. No change of personal leadership is possible unless I myself decide to change. Being able to change myself is also a necessity, if I want to control and influence others – without using physical violence. It is up to me to choose how I live up to my commitments and challenges. To stay where you are is sometimes quite pragmatic. The choice not to change is also a choice.

For the purpose of this book, I will use the concept *'dynamic leadership'* which stands for leadership behavior continuously chosen in an exchange process with the environment. It differs from *'instrumental leadership'*, through which the leader normally sticks to memorized principles and previously set rules. The conditions for leadership, whether dynamic or instrumental, can be described in terms of Task, Self and Team.

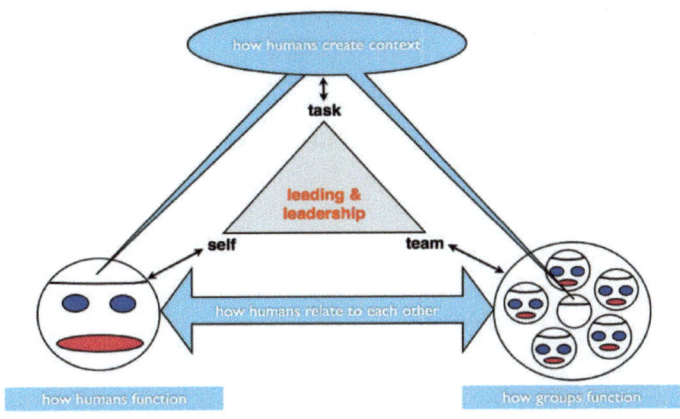

These three concepts will be further defined and elaborated on.

How I think as a leader is basic. However, leadership is more than that. In line with modern brain research I see thinking as an integrated part of holistic human being, rather than, like Descartes, separate from the physical body. The psychologist Manfred Kets de Vries emphasizes the importance of the leader's self-concept and it's influence on the environment. According to Kets de Vries, leading is a dynamic process in the encounter between the human being and the organization. In this process, leadership implies being in continuous contact with the task, the members of the team and one's self – in thoughts as well as through feelings.

In a formal leadership assignment special skills are required, that only certain persons have. However, I think that every person influences the leading process through attitude and behavior. In the following three sections, I will describe how everyone's ability to think, relate and influence can be enhanced in the leading process.

## 1.2    Thinking

*We develop leaders, and we develop countries. Or so we believe. We also believe that we develop countries by developing leaders. Perhaps we need to develop our thinking.*
Henry Mintzberg

The Monroe Institute offers a recorded introduction to one of their meditation programs that further confirms the importance of thinking:

*Science now knows much more about the combination of your mind, what and how you think and your actions, what you do and how well you do it. One fact stands out: if you think clearly, sharply, smoothly you will do and be far more effectively. If you direct your thinking, your thoughts, you can be whatever you so direct.*

How do we actually get something done? How do we accomplish change? According to the ancient Greek philosopher, Aristotle, wisdom comes first. He used the term *phronesis*, signifying 'practical intelligence', the ability to discern why and what to do – wisdom in action. He also asserted that *phronesis* is not enough. We also need to develop skills to actually do it (*techne*) and our ability to get results – to succeed.

There are many initiatives to contribute to a better future, and the will to change is often very strong. Methods for converting thoughts into actions are continuously being developed. Meditation, mental training, cognitive therapy, rebirthing, breathing and mindfulness are a few examples. Ways to become successful are continuously presented in management literature and by media. Most disciplines and organizations are engaged in continuous improvement and 'world class' programs.

There are, in my mind, two problems related to this development. The first is that wisdom, technological development and success courses are to a great extent driven by competition and egoism – from the reptile brain rather than from the frontal lobe. The second problem is that it is an externally controlled development, which does not enough liberate people's internal abilities, such as curiosity, creativity and the ability to create future visions. Both these tendencies cause gaps – gaps between ethics and action, between technology and actual success.

I think of three elements, which can fill these gaps – applied ethics, visions and innovations – all three examples of how we can use knowledge and thus challenge ourselves to learn more. By 'applied ethics' I mean regularly reflecting on what I am doing and on what I regard as good and right to do. Good visions, well reflected upon, can be the basis for radical innovations. However, for success, a lot of innovative work remains. The following examples show leadership through ethical, visionary, innovative – and patient – work in different contexts.

If you ask people to think of a visionary leader, the same names almost always are mentioned. Mahatma Gandhi's vision of a non-violent liberation of India is an example, which also inspired Nelson Mandela to his vision for liberating South Africa from the apartheid. In the business world Ingvar Kamprad (IKEA) and Steve Jobs (Apple) have already been mentioned. These leaders have acted in prevailing cultures of competition and fighting. To find examples of leadership in cultures of love and care I need to go back to Confucius, Muhammad and Augustine. However, these visionaries have been interpreted in ways that have led to long and violent fightings.

An interesting combination of ethics, vision and innovation, I find in Hässle, a Swedish pharmaceutical company, now a part of the Astra-Zeneca group. In this company, Ivan Östholm led development of new pharmaceuticals during three decades. Losec, a gastric ulcus medicine, has got most attention. In his book *Human Leadership* Håkan Lagergren interviewed Ivan Östholm.

Ethics stands for principles and values behind actions. They are as important for an organization as for individuals. Östholm tells us:
*Together we formed an environment in which it was obvious that we should develop pharmaceuticals that were good for humans with superior scientific and clinical documentation. Marketing*

24

*should inform doctors on how to use our pharmaceuticals proper-*
*ly. A creative atmosphere was an important condition: ideas be-*
*hind radical innovations are created by individuals.*

Perseverance was a necessity. According to Östholm,
the development of Losec took 22 years and in that period management wanted to close the project four
times.

The ethical goals were adopted in the 1950's. Losec
was launched in 1989 and has given the company more
than 50 billion euros in revenues.

These examples point at what is needed to develop our
ability to meet global challenges. Gandhi and Östholm
put ethics and *phronesis* first. They showed how sustainable ethical action can result in new options for people
and success for a nation state. Wise thoughts formed
the basis for visions needed for radical change and radical innovation.


## 1.3    Relating

*Trust is a fragile, valuable and invisible resource that is easily*
*damaged – it constitutes the most important part of the so called*
*social capital.*
Peter Stevrin (in my translation)

In order to take responsibility for the social system –
which I as a leader or collaborator have chosen to be in
– I need to understand how I am influenced by and influence people around me. This requires that I explore
how I *relate to others* and how *others relate to me*.

As a team leader I need to recognize how we relate to each other within the team and how we as a team relate to people and organizations outside the team. When it comes to human relating I will refer to the FIRO theory (see appendix 3). According to this theory my relations to others are dependent upon how much

- I include others?
- Others include me?
- I perceive others as significant?
- Others perceive me as significant?

- I control others?
- Others control me?
- I perceive others as competent?
- Others perceive me as competent?

- I am open to others?
- Others are open to me?
- I like others?
- Others like me?

For each of these questions, I might reflect on: 1) which answer I feel most comfortable with – my 'comfort zone' – and 2) how I behave when I am outside my comfort zone. This is the basis for my flexibility to act wisely in unexpected or emergency situations.

The next step in the analysis is about what is needed to fulfill the task and about the flexibility of people in the team and myself. If a certain task requires that two collaborators co-operate close to each other and the two of them avoid each other, there is a problem to be solved. If I control collaborators to such an extent that they do not act independently when needed, the team might have problems performing. If collaborators are not open to each other about problems they have, the consequences could be catastrophic.

In every organization there are daily problems, which need to be solved and are solved. Thanks to policies, rules, routines and instructions most of the daily problems are solved. The leaders and the collaborators find ways to relate to their task that work in most cases. Problems arise when something unexpected happens and the personnel involved do not manage to adapt their way of thinking and behavior. In situations like these the need for leading and leadership becomes acute. It is also necessary to have ethical goals well established as a basis for making quick decisions.

In unpredicted and emergency situations, flexibility is needed – that the leaders and the collaborators can adapt their behavior to what the current situation asks for. The leader has the formal responsibility for fixing and thus to be flexible in acting and relating. When there are conflicts among collaborators, the leader needs to rethink and adapt to what the situation asks for. Leaders that do not adapt should eventually be replaced. Replacing the leader is quite often the short-range solution. In a long-range perspective, routines and division of labor might need to be changed, but also that leaders and collaborators commit themselves to develop their relations and flexibility needed in unpredicted situations.

Flexibility might be limited by too much ego-fixation,

for example when persons rigidly stick to an attitude or a behavior in order to keep the job or to make a career. Also altruism can be a source of inflexibility – for example paying too much attention to other people and their needs. Intentional obstinacy can be very relevant and valuable, for example when life is at stake. However, unconscious and unreflected rigidity almost always causes problems in relations and limits the ability of the organization to handle unpredicted situations.

In their book *Living Leadership,* the consultants and organization researchers George Binney, Gerhard Wilke and Colin Williams write about leading as 'a social in-between activity'. They mention three things, which they found the successful leaders doing:

- *respecting* context and prevailing culture
- *relating* to the collaborators and having them perceive mutual responsibility
- *accepting themselves and respecting others* the way they are

According to these authors, the leader is in the middle of the team, rather than at the top. Above all, it is about people's ideas about roles – the role in the middle of, outside or in the top of the organization – and about the physical reality. A leader outside or at the top of a team does something *with* or *for* the team. Therefore, it is more about the mental than the physical position. Collaborators think of a leader who is 'always out traveling' or 'you never see'. A leader in the mental center of the team is in control – relations can quickly be tested an re-evaluated. This leader receives impressions and influences from within the team. The football coach is an example – being outside the field, but all the time in contact with the game and the players.

In this book, trust is one of three guiding principles for human action, the other two being meaning and power. In his book *Tillitskrisen (The Crisis of Trust)* Peter Stevrin writes that the importance of trust increases in the information society. Trust is crucial for how leadership can be exercised in an organization. Current management in organizations is often based on low trust. This is especially true for big and public organizations. This means leading through supervision and control. In these systems, the leaders tend to regard collaborators as parts of a mechanical system rather than as human beings whose devotion and creativity the system needs. *Engaging Leadership* – a concept used for instance by Henry Mintzberg and Antony Colijn – is based on trust.

Confidence and credibility are two aspects of trust. A leader needs to be trusted by the team members in order to stay in the middle. You gain confidence by being yourself and relating to others. Some people spontaneously give an impression of being trustworthy. Others need more time. Confidence is a type of capital to be maintained and cared for. In these days, the tempo is often so high that there is no time for building trust for the long-range. Teams and organizations often have short life cycles. Independent of whether trust is short-range or long-range, it can be lost very quickly. As examples from business and the public sector show, media can display circumstances, which can make a person completely loose public trust from one day to the next.

## 1.4 Influencing

*If I want to succeed in moving a person towards a specific goal, I first have to find out where he or she is and start from there. Genuine care starts with humility towards the one I want to care for and therefore I need to understand that helping is to serve, not to reign.*
Sören Kirkegaard (in my translation)

To lead means to initiate and making something happen – influencing. A leader has the responsibility to influence the social system the leader belongs to. This system is also an interactive network, in which all members influence and are being influenced all the time. How can a leader achieve wanted results through influence – achieve necessary changes? What is the meaning of personal leadership in relation to power and control?

To engage, motivate and act, are key leadership abilities. Trustworthy and influential leadership means having a personal way of engaging, motivating and acting.

When enough collaborators have had time to commit themselves to goals and meaning of the operations and trust the leaders, there is a climate in which power and control can be openly and constructively discussed. The individual's motivation to be influenced can range from loyally following without accepting to genuine acceptance of the goals of the organization. The issues of power and control are easier to handle when goals, meaning and motivation have been openly and straightforwardly treated.

Recognizing that we can be unconscious gives the leader legitimacy to make people conscious of circumstances deviating from the chosen course or threatening the trust. The leadership task is a formal duty. Ethics and trust are conditions that enable action. Deviations and distrust might require quick action – or, when there is more time – conscious creative work and agreements on adaptions and changes.

A leader may have different intentions, for example:

- to push in order to move on quickly
- to be a model for how to act in order to reach goals and visions
- to become aware of obstacles and unpleasant issues
- to complete actions or competencies that the team lacks

An important task for the leader is to engage and release the collaborators' energy, competence and creativity. By supporting and making them feel significant, competent and liked, the leader can show understanding of how humans function and trust their own potential.

Accepting human self-determination has a radical consequence: that I do not have any power to essentially change others. You are the only one who can change yourself. In order to avoid this dilemma we often tend to create new circumstances for people to relate to. Formal leadership means legitimacy to change circumstances within certain limits. The leader can challenge the collaborators and force them to choose. From this point of view the result of leading depends on both the leaders' and the collaborators' choices.

In this situation the leader's ability to motivate collaborators is extremely important. According to researchers Edward L Deci and Richard M Ryan, the most efficient motivation stems from inside each collaborator. Through leadership, the inner motivation can be stimulated. Perhaps the most important task is to motivate and support the collaborators to take responsibility for their self-esteem. This supports their ability to handle difficult situations and take responsibility for critical initiatives. It might require contact with the inner worlds of both the leader and the collaborator. It is important to point out that this contact with the inner worlds of others and yourself should be taken with extreme care and with love.

Thus, exercising power is efficient only when the leader's and the collaborator's own choices are being recognized and respected. A very dominant and charismatic leadership based on egocentric thinking could be a problem. Antony Colijn notices that *'these egos manifest themselves as large overpowering shadows in the organization'* making it difficult and uncomfortable for collaborators to take initiatives. Leaders should therefore make themselves conscious of their shadow in order to create space for their collaborators' capacity.

## 1.5    Self-Esteem

*The unexamined life is not worth living*
Socrates (in my translation)

In order to understand my relations to others, I need to understand how I relate to myself. This means working with my self-knowledge, becoming aware of my self-concept and taking responsibility for my self-esteem – how I choose to appreciate my self-concept. Again, it is about the three dimensions in the FIRO theory: Inclusion, Control and Openness.

To approach one's own self can be unpleasant and trigger inner defenses. Each of us has developed personal defenses against coming too close to our self – and to let others come too close. We need our defenses. They reduce fears and, sometimes, they can be quite relevant and valuable. Inability to handle fear might make people act violently and lead to undesired consequences.

However, the defenses are also like a distorted lens between me and other people. I am vague to others and I see others as vague. It seems that people's ability to handle and eventually avoid critical situations is dependent upon their personal defenses and and ability to handle their self-esteem.

'Self-esteem' can according to the dictionary be interpreted in at least two ways: 1) An inordinate or exaggeratedly favorable impression of oneself. 2) An objective respect och favorable impression of oneself. The second interpretation is the one to be used in this context. These two interpretations make self-esteem confusing and mirror the problem of appreciating myself.

In order to explore my self-concept in relation to leading and leadership, I need to collect and integrate information from different sources. For example, I can draw and explore my 'lifeline' of situations when I have perceived leading and exercised leadership. Every such situation is a source of self-knowledge showing different aspects of my way of relating.

Other approaches are:

- to consult a professional (psychologist, therapist, mentor, coach) who guides me to and through situations which might be hard for me to confront on my own.
- to join and participate in groups for dialogue or therapy, in which we explore our own and each others' experiences in contexts that we bring up.
- to ask for feedback from my collaborators, colleagues and friends.
- to use a psychometric or other written instrument for finding out how I have chosen to be up to now.
- to participate in leadership development activities – lectures, seminars and workshops.

What is the integrated picture I get of myself as a leader and how do I like it? How can I enhance my self-esteem as a leader?

If self-esteem is essential for the quality of leadership, it ought to be compulsory for the formal leaders to work with their own self-concept and self-esteem. In environments with extreme demands for safety, these requirements are explicitly tested, such as in the cockpit of an airplane or in a nuclear power station. There is a test for pilots, the *Defense Mechanism Test* (DMT) which explores childhood experiences, traumas, which could lead to undesired and risky reactions in critical situations. In other areas, such as health care and social services, deficiencies are being recognized and the requirements on the leaders and the collaborators are constantly being raised. After accidents and catastrophes the demands on the responsible persons are often subject to special attention and tightening.

In the program *The Human Element,* Will Schutz emphasizes the importance of self-knowledge and concludes that "a positive self-concept, self-esteem, is the bottom line". This is his invitation to the program:

*"I invite you to explore what happens when we do these things:*

- *Diminish our defensiveness and communicate openly and honestly with one another*
- *Diminish blame and acknowledge how we collude with one another to create what happens*
- *Diminish self-deception and allow ourselves to look inward and know ourselves well*

*The concepts are not presented as right or wrong or good or bad. They are concepts that may prove useful or not. It is in that spirit they are offered."*

## 1.6    In Search of Leading and Leadership

It seems that the human species continuously develop the abilities needed to confront changes in the physical environment and competition from other species – abilities to survive as a species. Probably the ability to co-operate has been developed for this purpose. Prerequisites for co-operation are built into the human organism and are transferred with the genes from generation to generation. Leadership is also a critical ability, but perhaps not coded in the genes, as seems to be the case with co-operation. However, I believe that fundamental factors in the leading process are inherited or developed early in life. The ability to think, the need for attachment and trust, the drive to control and the need for love and care are aspects of human life which research has confirmed to be a part of the child's repertoire from short after birth. This means that everyone might be born with pre-requisites for taking on different roles in the leading process.

My hypothesis is that processes of leading are going on in every social context, independent of whether we are conscious of it or not. By appointing formal leaders, the need for leadership in this process is being recognized. However, many situations and events in the world are outside the reign of formal leadership. This is the case in emergency situations, crises and other unpredictable events. Therefore each participant in a social context might need to contribute to the leading process by exploring, understanding and meeting the demand for leadership. Everyone has a unique potential to contribute. As was pointed out above, leadership requires flexibility to adapt to what the situation demands and thus probably to be outside the comfort zone. For this purpose there is a need for dedicated leaders who can complete what is missing. Not everyone has this capacity. Persons with this capacity often have early experience of leadership, which has given them opportunity to become aware of their self-concept and to practice taking responsibility for their self-esteem.

The dynamic perspective on leadership aims at finding the appropriate way of leading in a certain process. Intuition plays an important role and perhaps even more than the rational analysis. Intuietion is based on knowledge, which can be inherited or consciously trained. The road towards dynamic leadership goes via a conscious learning process.

This book offers ways of thinking – 'mindsets' – about this learning process. My intention is to use thought patterns to inspire you, the reader, to explore your own environments, your own basis and motivation for taking responsibility. First, the context will be described in terms of the physical environment ('the Task') and second in terms of the external and internal social context ('Self and the Team'). The next part is about how I can become aware and about interpreting, deciding and acting from what I am aware of. Maybe you want to try and deepen your knowledge in a concrete change process. My personal vision is a dynamic leading process, which supports the social responsibility that I think will be needed to confront global issues – a leading process as free as possible from directions and instructions. In the try-out phase there will be a need for instrumental instructions. However, instructions are only temporary supports – as the help wheels on a children's bike.

## 1.7    Pause for Reflection

The exercises in this book are intended to inspire you to use yourself as a reference in the 'search for leading self'. Your own self is the basic objective for this search. This is also the practice in The Human Element training.

Recall your own experiences from leading and leadership. You can do it by setting up your 'leadership lifeline' of experiences of being in groups.

- How was it to be a kid in the family in which you grew up?
- Your experiences from day care and schools?
- How was it in your leisure life, in sports, associations and meetings?

Which was your role?
Were you the leader or were you in the background?
Who took the leadership?
What did they do? How did you feel about what they did?

Choose a couple of situations from your lifeline.

- What was the meaning of the situation for you?
- Did you sense trust from the others?
- How did you influence the situation?

# 2 THE TASK

## 2.1 Sustainability

In the famous BBC television series about Planet Earth, David Attenborough reflects on the fact that the population of the Earth has gone from 1 to 7 billion the last 200 years. At present it increases with 2 persons per second and about 80 millions per year. One of the forecasts is an increase from 7.5 to 10 billion from 2017 to 2056. The increase is 2-3 times faster in the developing countries.

This forecast is based on the assumption that the current patterns remain, for instance that the current one billion teenagers reproduce according to what the economic conditions in the different countries predict. Assuming stable patterns makes forecasting population growth easy.

About seven generations have experienced continuous growth, growth made possible especially by the discovery of fossil fuels and the related technological development. This industrial period was preceded by the farming period, which lasted for about 10 thousand years, and during which the population was pretty stable around one billion.

In every period of development in human history there is sooner or later a limit to growth. One or more resources are getting scarce. These 'bottle necks' have challenged human creativity. For the first human beings the challenge was to find food for the day and in the close surrounding – the 'collection period'. Farming, fishing and cattle-breeding pushed human beings to move away to find nourishing coast lines and arable land. The competition for coast, rivers and arable land has been a driving force in the industrial period. Arable land is still a bottleneck. In the era of industrialism and high population growth, other resources have become scarce – such as clean water, energy and raw materials.

In the BBC series, Attenborough describes three challenges in the current development, perhaps the toughest:

- Food production need to double until 2050.
- The need for oil is calculated to increase by 40% the next 20 years. (NB: this was in 2011)
- One billion people do not have access to clean water.

Scarce resources are only one side of the problem. The uneven distribution of resources causes local bottlenecks to appear much earlier. William Reese is a professor at the University of British Columbia and the founder of the concept of the *ecological footprint*. According to Rees, each person on Earth needs access to about 4.5 acres of land. The industrial countries use 2-5 times more than that and the developing countries about 1.3 acres per person. If all human beings on Earth would have the same welfare as people in the industrial countries, we would need 1.5 planets.

It is a paradox that the uneven distribution of resources increases at the same time as conditions for a more even distribution are improved faster than ever. Transports and logistics systems, trade and money flows, and access to information and knowledge have all developed very fast the last century. Through technology and administration, we are better equipped than ever to establish an equitable distribution of resources on Earth.

Many of us are aware of the situation and many more have the option to become aware. Some think we are in a period of 'paradigm shift', an on-going fundamental change of our way of thinking and of the scientific basis for it.

On different levels in society the following simple questions can be formulated:

- What can we do and what do we want to do in this part of the world – in this region, city or municipal?
- What can we do and what do we want to do in this group or organization?
- What can I do and what do I want to do myself?

The answers are more complex. They are interrelated and need to be co-ordinated. The overarching contexts – nature, planet and humanity – can be described as systems in which the different parts contribute to the whole. Everything is dependent upon everything. Our ability to understand these connections has increased tremendously the last 50 years. Through cybernetics, systems theory and other applications of mathematics and logic, science has got new and efficient tools to describe and analyze complex contexts.

Scarcity and uneven distribution of critical resources also cause mental stress and physical confrontations. Individuals and groups have to fight harder to meet their needs at the same time as the number of options is reduced. Emotions tend to take control over the rational logic and sciences. Stress limits the creativity required to do something about the bottlenecks. The systems of economy and democracy tend to become the main objectives rather than means for distributing resources. The fights for preserving the systems turn into disagreements, open conflicts and wars. Instead of coordinating attacks on the bottlenecks, people tend to fight each other and with widespread destructions as consequences.

The extensive destruction all over the world has stimulated the quest for *sustainability*. 'Sustainable' means that something sustains over time and does not get destroyed or disappear due to temporary threats and human mistakes. In a UN report from 1987, 'The Brundtland report', sustainable development is defined as follows:

*to ensure that it meets the needs of the present without compromising the ability of future generations to meet their own needs.*

The needs can be divided into three categories – ecologic, economic and social – all interrelated to each other.

Sustainability can be met through systems. The systems need to be applicable today and by future generations. Especially, systems are needed in the transfer between generations, systems that guarantee options in the future. The challenges mentioned above are increasing through the quest for solutions that work also for future generations. Uncontrolled growth and exploiting finite non-renewable resources are examples of system consequences that are not acceptable in the future.

Accepting the challenge of sustainable development for future generations as a serious task and goal means that we need to do more: refining and developing knowledge, reconsidering and applying ethics and – most of all – acting. One important issue is to maintain the balance between abilities and challenges. Do we think that our collective ability can be developed to meet the new challenges or do we think that the challenges need to be reduced? What visions do we have? Do we think the end is close? Are we ready to take on the challenges and go from knowledge to intention and further on to action?

Using the term 'we' directs the questions to all levels in society. By replacing 'we' by 'I' the question goes to you and me:

- *What can I and what do I want to do in my part of the world – in my region, city or municipal?*
- *What can I and what do I want to do in my group or organization?*


## 2.2    Visions

It seems that we – human beings – survive by developing the knowledge and the abilities that we need as the populations grows and the challenges increase, thus maintaining a balance between challenges and abilities. In all shifts – from collecting to farming, from farming to industry and in the now on-going shift – people have developed abilities, tools and technical solutions to surpass the bottlenecks. To survive with lesser resources and at the same time increase welfare, humans have managed to change not only ways of living or life styles. Also the human functioning has changed in order to eat new types of food and to meet new physical situations.

The ability to survive is developed through knowledge. Knowledge is the raw material, which needs to be refined. This happens when knowledge is placed in new contexts and is being transformed to insights and conclusions. Refined knowledge can be the basis for wise action. Aristotle describes the quality of our action in three dimensions: Wisdom in action *(phronesis)*, Skills *(techne)* and Outcome *(factum)*. For transformation of knowledge to wise action, ethical guidelines are needed – how to reflect on what I find good and bad. For the development of skills and results, driving forces are needed – tension between the now and the future.

One way of transforming knowledge to power of action is to set up goals and visions. A vision can be intuitive from conscious and unconscious thoughts ('wishful thinking'). Phantasy sets the upper limit for our visionary thinking. Awareness of shortages and anomalies in the present sets the lower limit and is an important starting point for setting visions and goals. A vision can also be guided by our understanding of how things are interrelated and impact each other. Thus, we need both awareness and knowledge to create the tension between the now and the future.

As an example of a visionary vacuum, I would like to mention the global energy and our dependency on fossil fuels. Mats R Larsson points at the need for vision and power of action leading to a *Global Energy Transformation* during the 21st century. He gives two examples of radical visions implemented during the last century: The Marshall Plan for reconstruction after WWII and the American Apollo project resulting in the first human landing on the moon.

## 2.3    The Capacity to Think

The human race is one of millions of species on Earth and the species, which has developed the most advanced brain. The human brain has the capacity to be aware of and reflect over things happening inside and outside ourselves. During thousands of years we have developed a huge amount of knowledge about how the world and people around us function.

The brain is a workplace and a place in continuous development. Every second, the brain receives and processes an immense amount of signals. New connections between neurons – the synapses – are continuously created. According to recent research we continue forming synapses as long as we live – good news for us approaching the 'autumn of life'. In the brain, consciousness arises – a phenomenon which science cannot describe in terms of physical events – at least not up to now.

In addition to receiving information, the brain processes information, which has already been stored in memory. When there are no signals from outside the signals from inside take over. Those can be memories stored by earlier generations and transferred via the genes. Some images have been imprinted early in life and transferred to the unconscious in the background. Taking care of signals from outside and from memory – to make them conscious – is a vitally important and continuously on-going process in the brain.

By thinking we process conscious information from conscious and unconscious perceptions. It has been shown that we always try to connect our perceptions in order to form a meaningful whole. If there is something missing we fill it in with our phantasy. From perceptions in the brain we progress from thought to insight and further on to action and doing. We make choices all the time. How free we are to do that?

Philosophers have over time disputed whether we have a free choice (*determinism*) or if our thoughts and actions are controlled and predetermined by outside circumstances (*indeterminism*). Lacking the knowledge about how it really is, we can make an assumption on a scale from 'I have no choice at all' to 'I choose everything: my thoughts, feelings and actions'. My personal and current standpoint is that I to a large extent have a choice in issues concerning myself. I can choose how I relate to what is happening around me and inside myself. These choices can be well thought of and rational. They can be spontaneous and emotional. They can also be unconscious. However, unconscious choices can later be made conscious and related to. Making conscious choices and making choices conscious stand for using my capacity to think.

## 2.4    Emotional Intelligence

It is amazing to note that increasing awareness about the challenges, the quickly expanding knowledge and our capacity to think does not always lead to *wise* actions. There is an overflow of both challenges and brain capacity. Problems and conflicts are often left unsolved for long times – years, decades, sometimes centuries. You find them in the workplaces, in the local communities and on the global arena. These problems and conflicts also concern people outside the inner circle – all of us that receive information and get involved with our thoughts and feelings.

Lack of resources or technical solutions, secrecy, complex circumstances and locked positions are circumstances often used to explain why solutions and improvements cannot be achieved.

Quite often, anomalies are not approached until there is an accident – the catastrophe is a fact. There are different ways to postpone critical issues. Perhaps each of us recognize one or more of these examples:

- Facts are confirmed and left without action
  (-> passivity)
- Facts are confirmed and forgotten
  (-> passive secrecy)
- Facts are confirmed and put under the carpet
  (-> active secrecy)
- Facts are confirmed and subject to investigation
  (-> research)
- Action is initiated, but the parties dispute what to do
  (-> politics)

- Action is unsuccessfully tried and stopped
  (-> self-critic)
- Action is unsuccessfully tried, adjusted and tried
  over again (-> learning)
- Facts are confirmed and left to the market to solve
  (-> laissez-faire)
- Facts are confirmed and used by someone for profit
  (-> egoism)
- Facts are confirmed. Non-profit initiatives are taken
  (-> altruism, idealism)

Each of these behaviors can in a certain situation be relevant and reasonable. However, often I choose a behavior in order to avoid something unpleasant, for instance a feeling of fear, sadness or shame. Another reason can be worry for very strong feelings of lust or joy. Often, I am not aware of these 'emotional threats'. I choose my behavior unconsciously.

Modern brain research shows that at least two systems are working in the brain – the rational and the emotional. The rational system processes the conscious thoughts, the functions that we traditionally associate with the brain. The emotional system processes signals before they have reached the conscious. Often these signals help us to survive. That is when I want the emotions to be in control. Something suddenly approaches my head. I duck before being aware of what is threatening me. However, the emotional system can also take control in a unwanted way – when emotions are triggered by signals from inside, for instance from a traumatic situation in childhood. Pär Lagerkvist, a nobel prize laureate of literature, writes in his memoirs about when he as a child is digging a hole in the sand

and someone approaches him saying something like this: 'when you dig a hole in the sand, someone will die'. Short after that his mother dies. To dig a hole was for Lagerkvist a memory for life – also for myself and others who have read his memoirs.

Emotions control our behavior and our life much more than we believe – and often want. Feelings of joy and discomfort can take over. This can mean both possibilities and threats. Hardly anyone today believes that feelings do not exist or that they can be eliminated. However, the opinions differ about how the feelings can be controlled. Our public systems assume that we citizens can control our feelings and choose behaviors that comply with the laws. Ability to monitor your feelings – emotional intelligence – is a requirement on everyone.

## 2.5 The Power to Influence

Ways of thinking and 'prevailing culture' are phenomena deeply anchored in our communities. By the 'prevailing culture' I mean explicit and implicit visions, values and norms, which a majority of the people accepts and refers to as 'good' and 'right'. It is generally accepted that cultures differ between geographical areas and between social groups. Various attempts have been made to make certain values and norms accepted in all cultures, for example religious beliefs, human rights and respect for the environment.

Meeting the global challenges often implies that current paradigms and prevailing cultures are being questioned and changed. Thoughts and norms are often unconscious, such as thoughts, which prevent initiatives and change. They might have been around for generations in the unconscious. Mental obstacles are always inside myself on an individual level. Often, these obstacles have been hidden in the collective unconscious – in the current paradigm and prevailing culture.

A critical and difficult question is how to influence the current prevailing culture in order to open up for a sustainable society in all sectors and organizations. Maybe, if there are enough of us, thinking and feeling humans, who change our behavior? Meeting the global challenges also requires parallel changes in many different cultures.

In practice, changes take place all the time on different levels in society. Companies, municipalities, regions and other institutions establish plans for the future and follow them up. National parliaments and the European parliament decide on laws and decrees regulating our way of life and the way we relate to each other. On the global level, agreements between countries are made via international organizations such as UN, WTO and G20. In the civil society, new organizations and networks are formed all the time – Non Government Organizations (NGO) with the purpose to influence the decision in a direction wanted by 'the people'.

Behind every decision there are ideas and initiatives, which normally can be traced back to an individual or to a small group. Leading starts on the individual level and that is where a change of culture gets an initial direction. Soon after that, the collective power machine takes over. However, also in the collective system there are individuals acting, leading and pushing issues forward. It is in all talks and discussions in these processes that the current culture is formed. Every citizen takes part in this process influencing the collective conscious – and the collective unconscious.


## 2.6    Leading and Leadership

The collective consciousness can be regarded as a wave to follow and ride on. It is a flow that anyone can influence. Leading is a dynamic process in this flow which we can understand and deepen by exploring human functioning and interpersonal relations. Understanding is here to be referred to as the rational system – the capacity to think. Deepening refers to the emotional contact with the leading process – a deeper insight which can be reached through reflection and contemplation.

The continuous dynamics means that everything is moving in every moment. In every situation or context, we are included in a flow, which we have to relate to. The main direction is human development and survival of the species. The road is surrounded by challenges mentioned in examples above. I strongly believe that each human carries the potential to influence the processes – by taking initiatives and changing. We are more or less conscious of this potential. At the same time the flow carries an inner force and direction – the current culture and paradigm. The context is on the way somewhere and no individual has enough overview to see where is is going. The direction is formed by the history and the decisions here and now.

The notions of leading and leadership are used in many different contexts and signify a big variety of circumstances. My interpretation here is in terms of processes (leading) and roles (leadership), which are developed in every group of humans relating to the situation and to each other. Leading is a process of relating in which every person can participate.

From this point of view, it is relevant to explore how leading takes place in a certain situation and in a certain group. What does the group need in order to fulfill its task? The starting point is the roles that the members of the groups have been given or have chosen. Leadership in the group is a part of at least on of these roles. Where is the group going? What obstacles and challenges does it confront? Are the roles appropriate or do they need to be changed?

The development of machines, techniques and automation during the last 200 years has influenced our way of thinking about the human being. We tend to look for rational explanations of the way the human body and psyche work in order to understand how people are influence or are influenced by events. Humans can be given instructions how to behave in certain situations – in the same way as machines or robots. Many leadership schools assume that collaborators can be controlled and that the leader has the overarching control. This perspective is based on a mechanical-biological model of thinking about the human being – and on the myth that successful leading is completely rational.

Being convinced that the continuous dynamics need to be met by a dynamic leadership, I will here take the socio-psychological perspective on the human being. I will make use of the knowledge we have from biology, physics, chemistry and other sciences. The concept of 'dynamics' in leadership can be interpreted by metaphors from these disciplines. In order to be in touch with dynamics in the organization –sometimes very weak signals – I think the leaders need to go a little deeper into the personal inner world and get in touch with the emotional parts of their functioning and relating. Everyone is influenced by earlier experiences and decisions in the daily behavior. Every member of a group joins by bringing experiences and chosen behaviors from other groups. All these inputs influence the dynamics in the group.

There are many problems connected to the global development and these problems seem to be increasing. Wars follow each other and initiatives to meet the global challenges get locked up in political tumult. Management is very often regarded as weak or bad. A few persons in history are pointed at as very good, the clever and successful leaders – Mahatma Gandhi, John F Kennedy, Dag Hammarskjöld and Nelson Mandela being examples. Also persons like Adolf Hitler, Mao Tse Tung and Fidel Castro are leaders that have achieved remarkable results – whatever you think about their intentions and goals. After WWII, new leadership models have been framed by successful executives, such as Harold Geneen (ITT), Jack Welch (General Electric) and Steve Jobs (Apple). All these leaders have managed to make people work together and in the same direction.

When leadership can be connected to such a diversity of personalities and results, there is reason to ask if our conventional ways of thinking about leading and leadership are really useful in our attempt to meet the global challenges. Maybe the current paradigm shift will lead to a completely different way of thinking about leading and leadership?

## 2.7 Pause for Reflection

What is your role in leading for sustainable development?

1. Think about what sustainability means to you.

Define for yourself:

- Sustainable nature
- Sustainable human beings
- Sustainable organizations
- A sustainable society

2. What is the currently most important issue for you?

- in your private life
- in the community in which you live
- in the country you live in
- in the world, on the planet Earth

3. Recall a situation when you took the lead in an important context

In what way did you take initiative and intervene?
What made you act the way you did?

# 3    THE TEAM

*The Human Being's great advantage over other mammals and hominids is its capacity to build co-operating systems between different groups. They must have found a way to avoid territory fights and to replace rows between neighbors with collaboration.* Lasse Berg (in my translation)


## 3.1    Collaboration

The capacity of collaboration is evolutionary founded in the human organism. The genes developed over time in order to improve the conditions for survival. In his book *The Selfish Gene,* Richard Dawkins argues that the human 'darwinistic' adaption to the environment is continuously optimized on the genetic and molecular levels. He maintains that the genes are transferred to other individuals. Thus, altruistic interacting is a part of human nature and aims at supporting relatives, heirs and all others to pass on the genes. Our organs are made for collaboration. The notion of 'the selfish gene' is inconsistent, and Dawkins later changed it to *'the immortal gene'*.

Modern research on human functioning supports the idea that collaboration is biologically stored in the human organism. Mirror neurons enable communication – transfer of knowledge and co-ordinated action between people. The prefrontal cortex carries unique human capacities: to reflect on how to protect the self and to handle thoughts, feelings and actions towards others. Thanks to the language, we humans have a unique capacity to exchange thoughts, feelings and experiences with each other.

In spite of the fact that we are well equipped to care for others, it is not self-evident that we do so. In emergency situations, the inner parts of the brain take over in defending the self. It takes time and conscious effort to think about caring for others.

The contrast between egoism and altruism is always present and deeply founded in the human way of thinking. What some people regard as compassion is confronted with what others regard as self-interest and crass egoism. At the same time as I am supposed to ensure sustainability and survival of the human species, I have as an individual the duty to maintain my own life. The personal choices are not simple or straight-forward.

Both altruism and egoism have their motives. As the following example from navigation at sea shows, it is clearly not either-or. It is both. When a ship is in a critical situation, for instance in a storm, the order might be 'all hands on deck'. This means that everyone in the crew shall be available on deck. However, everyone has to make sure that one hand holds on to the boat to ensure one's own survival, while the other hand helps to save the boat and all the others in the crew. The one who falls in the water is lost. In practice, there are technical means to stay on board. However, everyone is expected to think of both oneself and the crew.

Each human carries a unique combination of capacities for collaboration. The inherited pre-requisites are complemented by experiences in life from living with other people in different groups and cultures.

In a group of people, these unique experiences meet. A 'group' signifies two or more people who for at least one reason are connected to each other. A 'team' is a group with shared specific goals, ethics or some other common aspect, which all members of the group are committed to.

The group is the first experience of social interaction. It starts in the primary family and continues in other groups, such as daycare, school, work, sports and various associations. My own experiences and conclusions have been framed in these groups.

The following three aspects give a logical perspective on the atmosphere and events in a group:

- processes during different 'phases' in the life of the group
- individual behaviors, thoughts and feelings
- how persons one-to-one relate to each other

Each group is dependent on each one of the participants. If one participant feels uncomfortable, the atmosphere and other aspects of the group will be affected - including performance and efficiency.

As participant I affect the group with my visible behavior and with my invisible thoughts and feelings. My behavior might not be consciously perceived by others. Anyhow, I influence the others' thoughts and feelings. Moving the team in a certain direction requires that I choose a behavior that the team needs. There are many alternatives and the team members are dynamically dependent upon each other. The choices I make might cause discomfort and inner resistance in me, which in turn can lead to bad atmosphere in the team. In order to understand and influence events in the team, I need to understand my own way of functioning – in other words: make myself aware of my self-concept and of how I feel about it.


## 3.2   The Self

*At the heart of all human functioning is the self*
Will Schutz


The self is already framed at the birth – perhaps even earlier – and it is influenced by the child's immediate contact with the surroundings. The child perceives being here and now, getting attention, reacting on others, receiving care, love or rejection.

The three stages suggested by Sigmund Freud – the oral, the anal, and the phallic stage – have been heavily questioned. Daniel N Stern, specialized in child development psychology, showed that the child starts developing all these stages short after birth. This means that important aspects of the self are formed parallel and not sequential. Continuously the profile is being formed of a mental me, my border-lines and the 'not-me'.

The child's early feelings of joy and discomfort are keys to understanding relational and group processes. People later in life bring these early experiences into adult relations and groups. Furthermore an individual trajectory is shaped by social background, cultural differences and life events.

Thus, an underlying structure is shaped early in life. It can be described as a number of basic assumptions or thoughts about the self, for example: 'people react on me – I get attention', 'nothing helps – I never manage', 'no-one likes me – I am not likable'. These unconscious assumptions in the underlying structure can later in life cause feelings of discomfort when I confront other people and different situations.

My basic assumptions frame my 'comfort zone' – here defined as the way to relate to others with which I feel most comfortable and secure. To manage outside the comfort zone, 'the security zone', requires conscious choices and efforts.

Will Schutz investigated different social contexts. He found that the way people relate to each other can be characterized in three dimensions. He set up a general theory – the aforementioned FIRO theory – about the driving forces and processes being around when humans relate to each other. FIRO stands for *Fundamental Interpersonal Relations Orientation*. Schutz claimed that the shaping of self takes place when people relate to each other – in the interpersonal field.

The FIRO dimensions represent three categories of psychological needs that people display in their behaviors and feelings towards others. The dimensions were originally described as follows:

1) *Inclusion:* to be together with others, include and be included
2) *Control:* to maintain order, to control or to be controlled
3) *Affection:* to give and get care, love, affection

These dimensions express behaviors. Later, Schutz changed the connotation of the third dimension from *Affection* to *Openness* – to give and get openness – arguing that openness is the behavior that displays the feelings of affection.

The emotional aspects of the dimensions are described as follows:

1) to perceive others as *significant* / to be perceived as *significant* by others
2) to perceive others as *competent* / to be perceived as *competent* by others
3) to perceive others as *likable* / to be perceived as *likable* by others

The comfort zone can be defined in each dimension as to what extent I prefer to

1) be together with others / include others
2) be in control / let others control me
3) show my feelings to others / accept others being open to me

Thus, there is a position in each dimension to which I tend to go, especially when being pushed or threatened.

The FIRO theory also describes my relation to my self, to what extent I

1) include myself / feel significant / am here and now
2) control myself / feel competent / determine my own life
3) am open to myself / feel likable / like myself

In this way I can explore my self-concept in terms of the FIRO theory. My 'self-concept' refers to the perception I have of myself. Later, especially in the sections 4.3 and 4.7, I will come back to the critical question: My self-esteem? – to what extent do I appreciate my self-concept?

## 3.3    The Human Elements

*I ignored 'the human elements' - personal fears, rigidities and defenses – in other words the real reasons why human events in organizations does not flow more smoothly.*
Will Schutz

The feelings and experiences I have of myself can be both joyful and unpleasant. In both cases, they can cause problems in my behavior and in my relations to other people. Both joy and pleasure can be so strong that I choose to avoid such feelings. Experiencing a feeling is an important source of information from my environment – for instance threats – and from my inner world – for instance when my self-esteem is threatened. Feelings are connected to body reactions in my heart, stomach and muscles.

Thus, the notion of 'feelings' used here has biological connections. Some experts apply the term 'emotions'. The philosopher Baruch Spinoza called them 'passions'. They are automatic in the sense that you do not have a chance to think before they appear. In the world of sciences, there are different opinions about which feelings are to be regarded as emotions. One of them, Robert Plutchik, suggests 8 basic emotions:

*fear - anger - joy - sorrow - acceptance - disgust - expectation - surprise*

One can make a distinction between basic emotions and more reflected feelings. The latter has been processed by our ways of thinking, consciously or unconsciously, and transformed to perceptions. These perceived feelings are more complex and combinations of different basic emotions.

It is common and very human that people choose to ignore their feelings and the connected signals from the body. This behavior has been and is in line with the current prevailing cultures. However, it is exactly this ignorance of important signals, which can have fatal effects on individuals, groups, organizations and society.

I mentioned how we in emergency situations can choose to stay in the comfort zone. When this choice is unconscious, we tend to be rigid – hold on to behaviors, which might be very inappropriate in the current situation. Typical signals of rigidity are that we do not listen and refuse to change – at the same time as the situation or the team might ask for a very different type of action.

In this situation, it is very critical and important how I manage my self-esteem – the feelings of joy and discomfort I have towards myself in the current situation. Taking responsibility for my self-esteem means letting myself be aware of my feelings, recognize them and recall where they come from – perhaps some early experience in my life. Recalling and identifying a situation in life when my self-esteem was low is a staring point for changing my current behavior – choosing one that is more relevant in the current situation.

We humans have an inherent capacity to react almost automatically when fear or other feelings of discomfort are stealing up. In psychology, they are called defense mechanisms or defense strategies. The basic purpose of these defenses is to protect us against real dangers and almost unbearable feelings of discomfort. There seems to be a limit for how much fear a child can stand. The defense mechanisms are therefore being developed in early childhood. Often, the discomfort is initially unconscious, which means that the defense mechanism is initiated before I am aware of the feeling.

There are quite a number of defense strategies – roles a person takes when discomfort is approaching. Here are some typical examples:

- Critic: Seeks, finds and points at mistakes others make
- Self-Blamer: Takes on responsibility for everything that happens
- Helper: Seeks and finds other people's problems
- Victim: Seeks and finds reasons to feel hurt by others

- Demander: Asks for more support and praise
- Denier: Maintains 'no problems'
- Fighter: Gets aggressive and attacks
- Withdrawer: Stays out and does not react at all

A defense reaction can be totally relevant in a certain situation and in a specific culture. The reaction can be totally irrelevant and destructive when it is triggered by a situation similar to one earlier in life. In the latter case it is supported by a basic assumption, concluded from what worked in the earlier situation. Unconsciously we tend to use these conclusions in the present situation.

Assumptions can be:

| + I am a significant person | – I am not significant |
| + I can cope | – I cannot cope |
| + I am a likable person | – I cannot be liked |

Thus, my basic assumptions and defense strategies co-operate on an unconscious level when discomfort and threat against my self-esteem are at hand.


## 3.4    The Team

A group is formed as soon as people get together and grow dependent upon each other. As the participants become aware of their dependencies and the group's relation to the outside world, questions arise how the group needs to relate to the surroundings and how the members need to relate to each other.

There is an analogy between the shaping of a group

and the shaping of self. Some scientific approaches to group dynamics have therefore used the growth of a child as a metaphor. Freud's ideas about genital stages initially inspired Will Schutz to look at groups as developing in stages. The original FIRO theory has thus been used as a theory of group development. However, it should be noted that Schutz clearly emphasized that he did not believe that there are distinct stages or phases and that each of the FIRO dimensions are relevant in every moment. This has also been proved to be the case for children – phenomena in all the three dimensions take place from the start of life.

Like many other Americans, Schutz had a dynamic approach to group analysis. The British tradition preferred a more static description of group processes. It maintained the aspects of the psychosocial 'structure', the communicative 'process' and the 'content' of what is going on in the group. The British approach seems to have had more influence from systems theory and cybernetics. There is more about information and less about energy.

The underlying structure of the team is mainly unconscious – collectively unconscious. It has influences from everyone who has been in contact with the group. As with the child's world of events, experiences and behaviors are stored in the 'group memory' – and frame a pattern of assumptions and conclusions. One of the most well known descriptions of the basic assumptions in a group was introduced by the British group-analyst Wilfred Bion. According to Bion, basic assumptions and connected behaviors in a group can be as follows:

DEPENDENCY – The leader is omnipotent. The collaborators feel inadequate and incompetent. The group is avaricious / greedy.

FIGHT FLIGHT – An outside enemy has been defined. The main objective is to defend and maintain the group. The collaborators are expected to sacrifice themselves for the group. The leader motivates them to do so.

PAIRING – There are pairs and other sub-groups. The main objective is to reproduce or create something new. The pairs are expected to fix it. No leader is needed.

TASK ORIENTATION – This is the positive opposite of the dysfunctional groups mentioned above. The collaborators are committed to the group's objective and on reaching the goals in the most efficient way.

Bion emphasizes that these are just examples. There are other combinations.

The development of the team is essentially dependent upon two factors:

1)  The basic and hidden assumptions.
2)  How the members relate to each other and how the group relates to the world outside.

Both these factors can be traced back to what the members contribute to the team and choose to do.

From relations and basic assumptions, conflicts between the selves in the team follow. The word 'conflict' means collision and encounter. Conflicts appear as a more or less unavoidable consequence of the different choices, which every team member made and currently makes. I think that this diversity of choices is an asset for the team. Thus, I regard conflicts between choices as something natural in a team – what the team needs to develop and what every team member needs to relate to.

Both the British and the American group traditions came out of the 20th century psychosocial, psychoanalytical and psychodynamic theories introduced by Freud, Jung, Adler and others. In the next section, I will show how the two group traditions, the dynamic and the analytic, can be seen together and as complementing each other.

### 3.5   Group Dynamics

The concept of 'Group dynamics' was introduced by Kurt Lewin, known for his fundamental initiatives in individual and social psychology. At the National Training Laboratories (NTL), Lewin in 1947 started 'training groups' (T-groups). Experiences from these group supported the idea that the group goes through similar stages as the new-born child. Lewin divided the group's development into three phases. In the first phase the group members are focused on authority, independence and inclusion, in the second on identity, mutual dependencies and control, and in the third on personal relations and trust. According to Lewin the phases can overlap and be repeated in cycles.

Group analysis was introduced and developed by S H Foulkes, founder of the Group Analytic Society. Foulkes describes the meeting between the group and the members in terms of 'localization' and 'the social matrix'. The members are the prominent figures who act on a scene ('localization') towards a background of a complex and total network of communication – the underlying structure, 'the matrix'. Each participant brings into the group a self with human elements and contributes to creating the norms of the group. The selves together contribute to an invisible and collectively unconscious web of relations and communications, 'the group matrix'. The group matrix is like the network of neurons in the brain. It can be seen as the operations center of communication in the group.

In every moment, there is a certain structure connected to the individual and the group. These structures are continuously exchanged and dynamically developed as the group develops. Every self is contributing to the norms of the group. Every self has to relate to the group norms. The visible content of these norms is continuously shifting. The process could be described as moving freely on a dance floor. Each participant in the dance contributes with an individual pattern of dancing. Each participant is being influenced by the rhythm and by the others' movements. The participants gradually make impressions on each other and frame common patterns on the dance floor. Changes in these patterns require individual initiatives and continuous communication.

In every group, there is a continuous exchange between the individual participants' self-identities. There is also a gradual development of the group's identity, the common culture of basic shared assumptions, norms and values. Using a metaphor from biology, one could talk about the DNA of individuals and groups. There is an exchange of DNA:s between the individuals and between the individuals and the group. These exchange processes might be as important for social development as the propagating process is for the biological development.

## 3.6    The Group Task

The task connected to a group makes the group a team. The task refers to what the team is expected to or wants to perform. It can have been allocated from outside or set up within the team. The task makes the dependencies inside the group more visible. The roles in the group become clearer and are eventually manifested by formal agreements. The task has a visible and an invisible unconscious part – just like the me and the team – with connections to the internal and external relations of the group. The issues are expectations, values and conspiracies related to the goal.

I would like to use S H Foulkes' model – a triangle picturing the team as a psychosocial system. The three corners and the matrix are here presented as an agenda for co-operation and leading in the team.

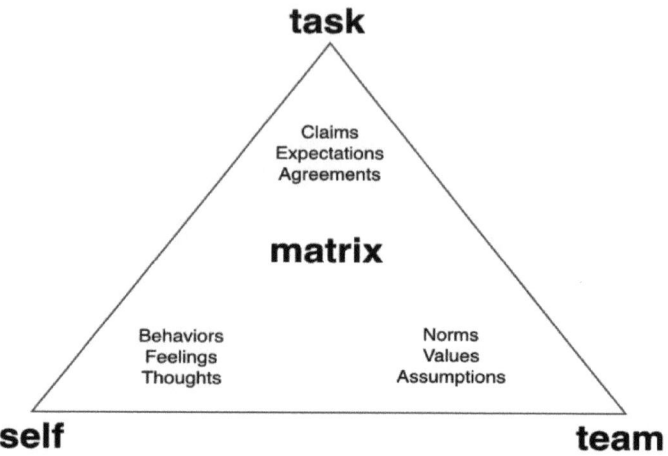

It is through this elementary system that individuals co-operate and influence their society. Everyone contributes to the matrix with combinations of behaviors, feelings and thoughts. In addition there are inputs from meetings, relations and communications inside the team and from the team's exchange with the outside world. This total exchange process repeats and is transferred from subgroups to organizations through the hierarchical levels of our society.

## 3.7    Co-operation and Conflict

Co-operation is manifested as individual needs in groups and teams. It seems to take place both among animals and humans. Possibly, the human capacity to think backwards and forwards is unique – to reflect upon one's own thinking.

The intention to co-operate is an important pre-requisite for co-operation. Jim Tamm and Ron Luyet explore this idea in their book *Radical Collaboration*. Our intentions are framed in a 'red and' a 'green zone'. The red zone is controlled from the inner parts of the brain and it mirrors egoistic behavior. The green zone is controlled by prefrontal cortex and stands for altruistic behavior.

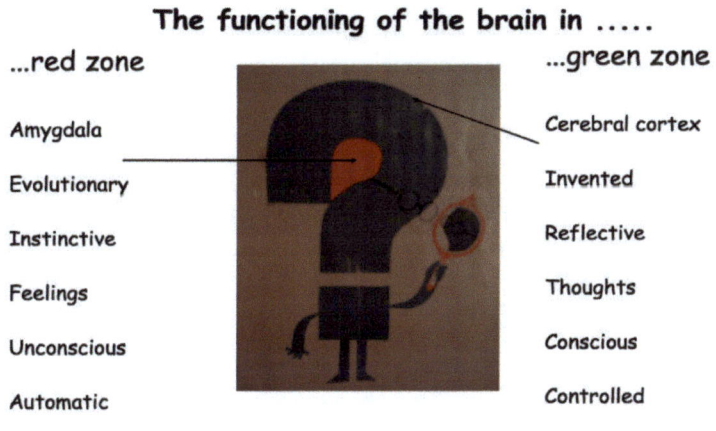

**The functioning of the brain in .....**

| ...red zone | ...green zone |
| --- | --- |
| Amygdala | Cerebral cortex |
| Evolutionary | Invented |
| Instinctive | Reflective |
| Feelings | Thoughts |
| Unconscious | Conscious |
| Automatic | Controlled |

x

Tamm and Luyet suggest a simple experiment to be performed with a group of people. The participants are asked to form pairs for arm wrestling. The rules are: 1) the one who pushes the other's hand into the table wins a point. 2) Get as many points as possible. 3) No talking! Every time I have asked a group to do this most of the participants have wrestled the traditional way – fighting hard for every point. A few recognize that you could just relax and let the arms swing together back and forth. This latter strategy gives about one point per second.

Most people choose to fight for individual success. This can be an unconscious choice since there is no time to think. Co-operation to win points together requires at least that you are aware of and recognize the idea to co-operate.

This simple experiment illustrates a paradox, which has been confirmed by scientific research. The human egoism is evolutionary built into the human brain, automatic thinking and unreflected behavior. Surpassing egoism requires conscious choices and time – time for reflection.

Our attitudes and intentions can be separated into two poles – competition and co-operation, egoism and altruism, red and green zones:

| RED ZONE | | GREEN ZONE |
|---|---|---|
| distrust | <--------> | trust |
| ownership | <--------> | sharing |
| withholding | <--------> | exploring |
| conflict | <--------> | concert, concord |
| unreflected speed | <--------> | time for reflection |
| a certain perspective | <--------> | many perspectives |
| either – or | <--------> | both |
| debate | <--------> | dialogue |

The intention to co-operate is not self-evident. The choice to co-operate requires being conscious of one's personal preferences and feelings of discomfort. To co-operate implies crossing mental borders – one's own and others'. The aim of co-operation has to be continuously recognized and questioned.

Much has been written about conflicts. Susan Wheelan points to the fact that research and development on preventing and solving conflicts has been given much more attention than co-operation. It seems that we have a tradition of thinking more of conflict than of co-operation – at least in the Western societies. The red zone is a symbol of a main theme of history. In spite of the fact that conditions for co-operation are built into the human organism it seems that fighting spirit has dominated through the major part of human history.

My own experiences and conclusions confirm that both conflict and co-operation touch my fears and other discomforts towards something I tend to avoid. My aversion against conflict is often the fear of escalation, aggression and violence. Co-operation is confronted by my fear of ending up outside the comfort zone – for example my fear of getting too much or too little attention, my fear of being asked to lead and eventually loose my face or my fear of being rejected. There is also discomfort triggered by seeing others being outside their comfort zone.

My perception of myself in the company of others influences how I perceive myself. In my view, this is a basic pre-requisite for human co-operation. Having a realistic self-concept – the capacity of handling feelings of discomfort and taking responsibility for my self-esteem – helps me going in and out of groups with more openness and sense of responsibility. Being inside a team, my task is to recognize and understand the need for leadership – as well as how to relate to members and complete the group. By doing this I maintain and develop my capacity to contribute to efficient and human co-operation in the team.

When my self-esteem is threatened, I could try to make myself aware of what is going on, process my awareness in order to understand and initiate change. This implies confronting myself and questioning my own behavior. It is important to do this in a considerate and caring way. It might be wise to ask for advice from relevant others. To let the unconscious out and relate to what is coming out is a way to handle the dynamics in my meetings.

## 3.8    Pause for Reflection

Explore your own experiences from being in a group or in a team. Select a workgroup/team that you belong to or have belonged to.

1.  Describe the team's task
    - Commitments the team has made
    - Expectations on the team from outside
    - Agreements within the team

    Reflect on the efficiency of the team.

2.  Make two lists of current issues

    A) issues which are openly addressed
    B) issues which are not addressed, at least not openly

    Reflect on how the A- and B-issues influence the efficiency of the team.

3. Describe the team climate/atmosphere in terms of the FIRO dimensions:

- To what extent do you include each other, do things together?
- To what extent do systems, rules and managers control your performance?
- How open to each other are you? How caring?

Reflect on how well the climate meets the requirements of the task.

4. Analyze your own experiences in the team.

- Your role in the team and how you perceive your influence on the team?

- How satisfied are you with yourself in the team?

- Situation in which you have been worried or afraid?

Reflect on your behavior when being outside your comfort zone.

# PART II

# DEVELOPMENT

# 4    AWARENESS

## 4.1    Consciousness

The notions of 'conscious' and 'unconscious' are problematic, partly because science has not found a satisfactory theoretical explanation of consciousness. The unconscious has been scientifically explored for at least the last 200 years. In this, the industrial period, philosophers, psychologists, neuroscientists, brain researcher and others have developed a general understanding of how humans can become aware of themselves. One conclusion is that the exchange of information between conscious and unconscious goes via overlapping states of awareness. There is no sharp borderline.

The word 'conscious' comes from Latin *conscientia* meaning 'with knowledge'. In Greek the word *suneidesis* is used meaning 'common knowledge' – knowledge together with others. Up to the 18th century the Greek meaning dominated. The religious demand for good and right thoughts – ethics and morals – was in those days high up on the human agenda. The idea of being unaware was taboo because it deprived humans of control of their own life and of their moral responsibility. This religious dominance was broken by the acceptance of science and through the development of philosophy. The interpretation of 'conscious' changed from 'knowledge together with' to 'with knowledge'.

The philosopher René Descartes (1596 - 1650) has had great impact upon the Western view of consciousness. With his famous statement *Cogito ergo sum,* 'I think, therefore I am', he concluded that there are two types of events in the world: those with physical extension (matter) and those without (thoughts and other spiritual phenomena). For 400 years, this dualism has influenced the Western way of thinking in both science and religion. Consciousness is identified with awareness and thinking. Via Descartes the idea of consciousness was transferred from the social to the individual aspect of human life.

Through modern brain research new connections between physical activity in the brain and mental perceptions are continuously being discovered. These insights have changed our common view of consciousness and have caused some scientists to question or reject Descartes' dualism. No specific place for consciousness in the brain can be identified. There are activities going on in different places at the same time. There is also communication between human brains via the mirror neurons – a discovery supporting that consciousness is framed in the social field between humans – maybe completely dependent upon humans relating to each other. Perhaps, the time has come for transferring focus back from the individual to the social?

When it comes to understanding of and influencing human functioning, the distinction between conscious and unconscious has important practical meaning – for example for how we learn and solve problems. It is well known that we soon forget and become unaware of what we once read or saw. Through repetition knowledge becomes conscious and easier to memorize. When I do things that I am familiar with, I normally do them more or less unconsciously, for example biking and driving. Once I begin reflecting on how I do it, the risk for making a mistake increases.

Consciousness cannot be univocally described. In order to get an overview, different perspectives are needed. I will refer to the following three perspectives on what happens when we become aware and on how to become aware:

1) **The physical-biological perspective**
   focusing on the consciousness processes in our brain

2) **The psychological perspective**
   focusing on the individual behavior and the consciousness behind it

3) **The social perspective**
   focusing on what happens when people relate to each other in groups – collective behavioral patterns developing in social contexts, patterns which might have been passed on from generation to generation.

## 4.2    The Physical-Biological Perspective

Important contributions to our understanding of consciousness come from the brain research, especially in the last 50 years. It is now possible to observe physical events in the brain related to specific mental processes. Through functional magnetic resonance imaging (fMRI) it has been made possible to see what parts in the brain are activated when a person feels, thinks or acts. The results indicate that a mental process activates the brain in many different places at the same time. For instance, recalling a memory involves co-ordination between different regions in the frontal cortex.

It is now generally accepted that there is conscious and unconscious knowledge, that the flow of knowledge is controlled from the brain and that the unconscious dominates over the conscious. Signals from the brain are transferred via the nervous system to receptors in the organs. There are two types of input to the nervous system: physical-chemical and psychosocial. Through unconscious activity in the brain the information is evaluated, sorted and rinsed before it is made available in the frontal cortex for conscious evaluation, planning and action. The major part of the information from outside is directly transferred to action without passing the consciousness process.

The human brain weighs around 1.5 kilo and comprises about 100 billion neurons. Each neuron is via synapses connected to up to 10 thousand other neurons, thus framing an enormous network. There are also about one trillion glia cells supporting and protecting the brain.

In the physical-biological perspective, it is practical to divide the brain into three sections:

I    The inner parts – thalamus, hypothalamus and cerebellum – having the co-ordinating functions. Thalamus receives and transfers information about temperature, pain and touch. Hypothalamus automatically controls the autonomous functions in the body – such as breading, heart beating, sleeping, hunger, thirst, body temperature and sexual instinct.

II    The limbic system or paleo cortex – especially amygdala and hippocampus – regulating and transferring emotional experiences. Here, the basis for behavior and action is framed, signals which are directly transferred to the body organs or processed by the outer parts of the brain. All threatening signals pass amygdala, in which fear and other feelings of discomfort are initiated. Amygdala stores early and unpleasant memories for conscious processing later in life. Hippocampus makes it possible to recall and re-experience these and other memories.

III   The outer parts of the brain, cerebrum, consist of a number of lobes. Most important is the front lobe, prefrontal cortex, the latest and the most developed part of the brain. Here major activities of the brain are co-ordinated – for example: attention, memories and thoughts – and the unique human functions of self-reflection and will. The front lobe has a left and a right hemisphere. The left hemisphere controls the right parts of the body. Here, sequential processes are controlled, such as language. The right hemisphere controls the non-verbal processes. The hemispheres are normally in contact with each other and complement each other.

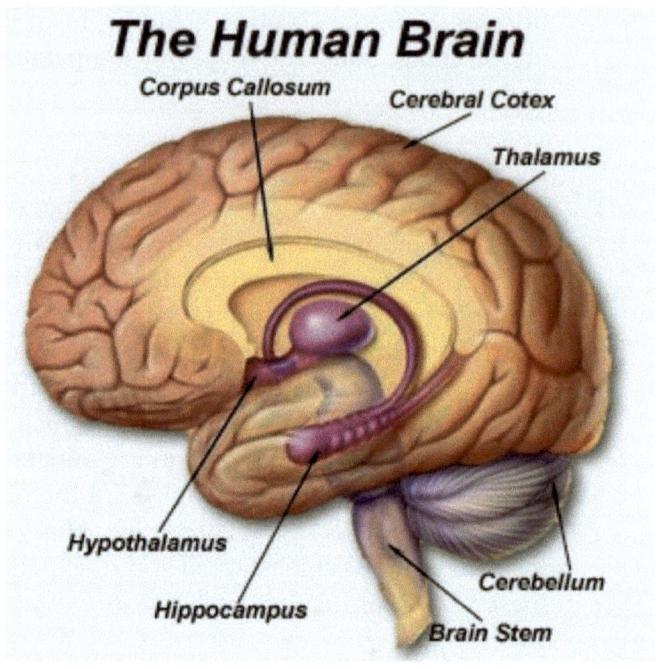

# The Human Brain

Corpus Callosum

Cerebral Cotex

Thalamus

Hypothalamus

Hippocampus

Cerebellium

Brain Stem

In the consciousness process, signals are transferred from outside to the senses (sight, hearing, taste, smell, touch), from physical vibrations in the organs to electro-chemical signals in the neurons. Incoming signals are compared with those stored in the memory. Our behavior is controlled by electro-chemical signals via neurons and synapses and by hormones.

Sudden danger or threat short-circuits the consciousness process. Signals are then triggered directly from the inner and the limbic systems. When there is time for it, the outer brain and consciousness will be connected.

Some of the discoveries in modern brain research are especially important for understanding and influencing consciousness and will.

The synapses constitute the brain's capacity to adapt to the environment and its demands. During the child's first year a great amount of synapses are created – at the age of one about 1 million per second! The synapses needed survive and the others are destroyed. The unique human capacity for speech and language develops in this process. Creating and destroying synapses go on through life. Even old people adapt the configuration of neurons and synapses.

It has been shown that also our genes change during our life time. According to 'epi-genetics', genes can be turned on and off. Every cell contains the whole unique set of genes. Individual genes can conditionally be turned off and reactivated. This could be the case when digesting specific foods and reacting on physical contact with certain chemicals. This 'epi-process' goes on through our whole life and is especially intense during the first years.

Mirror neurons give a biological explanation of the fact that we can imitate others and understand others by watching their behavior. They were first discovered in monkeys. These neurons are activated by certain actions and when the monkey sees someone else perform the same action. The mirror neurons also exist in human beings and seem to develop in early childhood, eventually already at the age of six weeks. The discovery of mirror neurons explains the development of self, both from a psychological and a social perspective.

An interesting relation between the conscious and the unconscious was quite early demonstrated by brain research in a questioned experiment. In 1964, Lüder Deecke and Hans Helmut Kornhuber showed that an unconscious electric signal precedes a physical activity – the *'bereitschaftpotential'*, a signal saying 'now I am ready'. This signal is initiated about 800 milliseconds before the activity. Later, Benjamin Libet showed that the conscious intention behind the activity takes place 200 milliseconds before the activity – clearly later than the 'I am ready' signal. What influence does consciousness have when coming in that late? One could conclude that we actually do not consciously control our actions. However, that is not in accordance with our experience and the assumption of free will. Libets suggested that we consciously can control the action before it is performed. The activity is prepared in the unconscious but has to be released by the conscious. I cannot consciously prevent the activity from being initiated, but I can prevent it from beingcompleted.

A practical method to increase awareness has been developed by the Monroe Institute in USA. In the 1950's, Robert Allan Monroe discovered that sound with certain combinations of frequencies influence the state of awareness. The Monroe Institute has developed this discovery to a patented technology, HemiSync®, in which low sound frequencies are used to stimulate different states of awareness in the brain. It has been shown that an even distribution of activity between the two hemispheres increases the capacity for awareness, such as the capacity for attention and the capacity to remember.

The ability to relate develops from early childhood. I have personally experienced communication with my grandchildren at the age of six weeks – observing that their mirror neurons receive and responds to impressions from my body and face movements. When the child can recall memories, conscious learning is definitely on the way. The actions of the child are registered through the creation of synapses and neurons, and also through the genes being on or off. It is certainly not possible to register and control everything going on in the child. However, it is clear that we adults have the possibility to influence the child's life and learning environment, especially when the child relates to us.

The capacity to think develops early in life and later on in school. Therefore, I do hope that modern knowledge of consciousness will be actively and systematically applied in the teaching methods of my grandchildren – for instance, knowledge about the memory, how we learn new things and remember them.

From early childhood, we also learn how to control and influence our surrounding. The capacity to control develops all through life. For instance, I can learn to stop initiatives that my brain sometimes unconsciously suggests. My synapses, neurons and genes can always be influenced by my consciousness via my continuous learning and training. Of course, I have to make a reservation for the fact that people's physical and biological circumstances can be very different.

## 4.3    The Psychological Perspective

*The best solutions to organization and leadership issues require self-awareness as an essential first step. Deepened self-insight leads to self-acceptance and then to self-esteem.*
Will Schutz

By 'self-insight' I mean conscious knowledge about my self – personality, inherited and learned capacities, ways of functioning and reacting in different situations. The self-insight represents a unique flow of thoughts, feelings and behaviors.

The notions I, me and self, are often interpreted as identical or interchangeable. Sometimes it is practical to make a distinction. With 'I/me' I refer to the active part that is acting out. The 'self' connotes what is inside. With this distinction the self is the existential basis for I and me. The I relates to others and self.

My self-concept is the basis for my self-insight – conscious and unconscious thoughts that I have about myself. By definition, unconscious thoughts have been conscious at some time. My self-concept is the result of my personal history and experiences from birth up to now. Self-insight is framed by conscious interpretation of my experiences and conclusions from how I behave and function in different situations.

Handling my self-insight means that I make myself aware of and explore my self-concept and arrive at new conclusions. More self-insight means that I am closer to my 'real' self. It seems reasonable that self-insight can increase and decrease. My experience of inspiration and satisfaction in contact with others and my self tells me in what direction it goes. Self-insight goes up and down together with self-acceptance and self-esteem.

A point of reference for self-insight is what I call 'the inner core' – the 'real' self that has continuously been framed since it was born. There are biological and psychological reasons to protect the inner core from being in contact with others and with my conscious self.

Fear is a major component in this human protection system. Through fear, information about threat is transferred via the brain to the whole body. When there is an emergent need for action, the signal goes directly to the muscles. The fear is not even perceived. When there is more time, the signal is sent to the prefrontal cortex to be interpreted by thoughts. Now I am aware of the fear and it can be a basis for conscious action. The conscious fear could be unbearable. There is a limit for how much fear a human being can stand. Therefore, there are other protection components available – defense mechanisms – to reject the fear and the thoughts connected with it. Well trimmed, these mechanisms can start acting before the fear becomes conscious. Even if the situation is not urgent, a quick and unconscious action might be initiated.

In this way, layers of protective thoughts and behaviors are safeguarding the inner core. A new aspect of the self-concept is connected to each layer – a preprogrammed way of thinking and behaving. Some of these layers can be hard to reach via consciousness, like the inner core itself. As we have seen, these hidden parts of the self-concept could be biased and contribute to misconception of the self. Even if these layers originally are framed in order to protect, they might later on be more and more irrelevant for the task to be performed.

Going deeper, processing and rinsing the layers around the inner core, can be a shocking and painful experience, but also associated with a strong feeling of freedom and happiness. The inner core is like a heap of stones. When a certain stone is taken away, there is a sudden slide. When the other stones have found their new positions and are in balance, there is a tangible moment of tranquillity in the heap. Lifting the stones in our personal heaps – carefully and with love! – is a way to find solutions of our human problems – personal, others' and common problems.

There are a number of sources I can go to for the purpose of exploring my self-concept, for example the following:

- Feedback from others about how they see me
- Feedback to myself – how I see myself
- My fantasies and dreams – can be reached through (guided) visualization
- Instruments for self-evaluation based on scientific research
- Body experiences – can be reached through specific movements designed to bring my body in touch with myself and with others.

These and other sources complement each other by adding different perspectives on my self. Each source can bring new and valuable knowledge of the inner core. Each source is also subject to distortions. There can be distortion in the original signal and in my interpretation of the signal. It is therefore valuable to be open to signals from different sources and to question each of them with respect to relevance and precision. It is the me that makes the final judgement. It is the me that becomes aware and arrives at self-insight.

## 4.4　The Social Perspective

In the previous chapter, the presence of all the selves in a team was described as a social matrix. In the social matrix of a group, the members' self-concepts meet and shape patterns of expectations, values and agreements that are unique for each group. This matrix represents an underlying structure of unexpressed norms and practices. The structure influences how people behave, communicate, and express their thoughts and feelings. The content of the structure is unconscious as long as the issues are not made conscious on the common arena of the group.

Carl Gustav Jung coined the notion *'the collective unconscious'* representing a universal innate psyche in everyone. When unconscious, it is a common asset. When consciously expressed, it also becomes something personal. The different personal ways of relating to the matrix are like different ways to cross deep waters containing more or less dangerous obstacles on and underneath the surface. You can learn to navigate in order to avoid the obstacles. You can also choose to go deeper and explore the obstacles in order to change them or eliminate them. Whatever you do, you need to know where the obstacles are.

The prevailing culture in a group or in a community is like this underlying structure of patterns – language, values, norms and institutions – being transferred from generation to generation. Some aspects of the culture are clearly manifested and can be directly experienced. Culture also changes over time. Like in groups, most of the cultural heritage is underneath the surface. Attitudes, values and other forces behind behaviors are hidden and are constantly being (re-)framed.

Power is an expression of cultural innate patterns – how power is understood and exercised. The social sciences define at least three aspects of power. One is the capacity to control and win, for instance in a decision process. A second aspect is the power to set the agenda – to propose and withhold issues. In this way, some issues might be out of the common collective consciousness. As a consequence of this, the third aspect arises: the power of the current prevailing culture. It is no longer a certain person having the power. The power is hidden in the underlying structure of the community. The 'normal' is taken for granted.

Earlier generations' attitudes to power and authorities often stay in the prevailing culture, especially via the religion. In Sweden, Protestantism was introduced by the king Gustav Vasa, and we can still see the norms of discipline and work morals which were established in the 16th century. From the beginning of the 13th century the roman-catholic church exerted the power of violent inquisition. This institution was around up to 1908 and there might be remainders of inquisition in our current secret services.

The foundations of our social perspectives are laid in early childhood. The family is for most of us the primary group. August Comte suggested in the 19th century that the human race could be regarded as a continuous development from the individual family. He and others conceived that we bring our early perceptions from the basic family to different groups that we belong to later in life – for example child groups, school classes, associations, political parties, work groups and management teams. The personal comfort zone of fundamental needs for inclusion and acknowledgement, control and power, care and love, are shaped in the family and remain the starting point in future contacts with community.

As time goes it gets more and more difficult to connect to and do something about the collective unconscious. The difficulty increases with the size of the group. The larger a group is the more mental resistance will be around preventing a participant from raising an issue, especially if the issue is about relations and climate in the group. The problem is visible in a large group (> 50 people), in which the distance between some of the participants can be big and it can take a long time to get reactions and feedback from the others. Still, the resistance is primarily appearing inside each participant as a strong feeling of frustration against taking initiative and intervening. This resistance has to be overcome in order for the structure to be influenced and changed.

The larger the group is the larger the frustration and the fear to speak and show feelings openly. In small groups (< 15 people), it is much easier to establish a secure atmosphere. In a median group (15 - 50 people), the frustration is more obvious. It takes more time to get feedback and in the waiting period, there is uncertainty. In large groups, the feeling of anonymity takes over. Attention is unevenly distributed and the competition for control and power is fiercer. Insecurity and frustration in any group tend to increase as some participants move outside their comfort zone.

As time goes on, the group assembles more history to handle. The process of information handling in the group is similar to the corresponding individual process. Events, experiences and signals are stored upon each other shaping a collectively unconscious group memory. The memory gets more divided and fragmented as signals are stored in different participants – like information is stored in different places in the brain. In stable groups, structures might develop which facilitate open communication and make it possible to contain the frustrations. These groups might reach a state of trust and solicitude.

The collective unconscious is stored in the unconscious memories of the individuals. It can be made available when people meet face-to-face and take their time to explore their memories on a deeper level. In the same way that individuals and groups grow in contacts with their inner core, a community grows. In organizations and communities, this awareness process has to take place in large groups in which a great number of memory images are represented.

## 4.5  Handling the Unconscious

In order to influence a context, I need to find out how things work and how they are connected. Since I cannot reach 'the thing-in-itself' *(das Ding in sich),* I need to explore my own and others' perceptions of how it is — inside myself, in my relations and in the social contexts that I am a part of.

I will assume that I have used the aforementioned sources and methods and that I am aware of my current social relations. In order to test the quality of this information, I can use the following checklist:

- What have I seen and heard of others' behavior towards me?
- Which are my own fantasies?
- Which are others' unexpressed feelings and intentions?
- What do I feel in the presence of others?
- Do I make myself aware of everything that is important in my relations?
- Is there something I am afraid of?
- What is the worst that could happen?

These questions pay attention to my resistances against being aware and to how I protect myself against unpleasant perceptions. Am I outside my comfort zone? Is my self-esteem threatened?

The way I relate to others has to do with how I relate to myself. When seeing myself in a mirror I can ask myself the same type of check questions as above:

- How do I behave towards myself?
- What do I feel in my own company?
- What in myself evokes feelings?
- Which are my feelings towards myself? Pleasant? Unpleasant?
- Is there something in myself that I am afraid of?

Exploring a social system is more complex. As we have seen, the circumstances in a group are more or less hidden in the matrix or web of complex relationships – participants' history, interpersonal relations, silent agreements and personal agendas.

One way of making the collective unconscious conscious is through dialogue. The notion of 'dialogue' comes from Greek *dia logos,* "through words, through meaning". Dialogue works as a link between the individual conscious and the complex group matrix. It differs from other ways of communicating by giving space for both thoughts and feelings. Fragments of the collective unconscious are brought to the surface and made conscious to the whole group. Dialoguing supports the group in discovering new meaning and something that almost everyone in the group can consciously relate to.

In larger social systems – such as companies, institutions and public organizations – other exploration methods are needed. In order to understand the needs of the system, one has to explore the history, the present and the future plans of the system. The daily communications are important inputs – as between collaborators, in the management team, in the board and among owners. Which are the problems and possibilities being discussed? Often, external consultants are recruited to map the current situation, make a diagnosis and give feedback. Additional sources of information are the internal perceptions of the organization, feedback from external connections and self-evaluation instruments, such as climate or culture analysis.

The purpose of a climate analysis is to describe how the members of the organization look at the situation as a collective and how they want it to be. The climate analysis does not track individual positions and it does not evaluate whether a position is right or wrong, good or bad. The result of climate analysis is one out of many different contributions to the understanding of the underlying structure. It can support a dialogue on what can be done in order to make the climate of the organization more human, productive or whatever the current situation requires.

## 4.6   Integration of Perspectives

Debates and discussions are often about which perspective is right or true. The positions are often based on sciences and beliefs. Reductionism aims at reducing the explanation of phenomena to one or a few factors – when it comes to consciousness to a physical-biological explanation. Mysticism and religions rather assume that there are no scientific-rational explanations and that there are always irrational components. In the field between reductionism and mysticism, there seem to be positions that strive to integrate the different perspectives. Ken Wilber's integral model – *The Integral Approach'* – is an attempt to understand everything in a holistic context. The model has five different 'elements' which are supposed to make it possible to include a great variety of perspectives:

- *States* of consciousness - being awake, dreaming, deep sleep

- *Levels* of development of human consciousness

- *Lines* of development – cognitive, emotional, esthetic

- *Types* of humans – personalities according to different typologies

- *Quadrants* – perspectives: Me, We, It, Those

The four quadrants represent the first, second and third person perspectives. They correspond to the three perspectives in this chapter: the psychological, the social and the physical-biological. According to Wilber, processes in the four quadrants always run parallel. Descriptions and theories of what is going on can often be included in at least one of the four perspectives and thus complement each other.

|  | The internal world | The external world |
|---|---|---|
| **i n d i v i d u a l** | **1st person**<br>**ME**<br><br>psychological<br>mental<br>subjective | **3rd person singular**<br>**IT**<br><br>physical<br>biological<br>objective |
| **c o l l e c t i v e** | **1st & 2nd person**<br>**ME & YOU = WE**<br><br>psychosocial<br>relational<br>culture | **3rd person plural**<br>**THOSE**<br><br>community<br>organizations<br>systems |

The line between the internal and external world can be regarded as a symbol for becoming conscious. This is where the inner mental perceptions meet the impressions from outside. From the biological perspective, we can imagine that the signals being triggered from outside go to the brain, where they are being compared with signals from stored memories. From the psychological perspective, it is me as a person who shapes my images of what is going on outside. From the social perspective, it is we relating to the social systems in which we perceive we are.

The integral model invites different perspectives to be included. It offers a language through which we can relate ideas and concepts to each other. The model also supports a dialogue between people who are conscious of a certain perspective and want to understand each other.

## 4.7 Pause for Reflection

An application of Ken Wilber's integral model.

Choose a current event in your life.

Recollect your observations and reflections from this event – facts, thoughts and feelings.

Place each observation in one of the four quadrants:

(1) the individual internal – the psychological perspective
(2) the individual external – the physical-biological perspective
(3) the collective internal – the underlying structure
(4) the collective external – systems and organizations

Reflect on the meaning of the content of the different quadrants.

Reflect on how your observations might be connected with each other and how they might be mutually dependent upon each other.

Try to become aware of something you did not think of before.

Summarize your interpretations of what you see.

# 5 DIALOGUE

## 5.1 Relating to the Conscious

This chapter is about how we can relate to what we have become conscious of. Again, the dialogue format is useful. In the former chapter, dialogue was introduced as a way to become conscious of and see the meaning of what happens. Now I want to use it for interpreting what happens, to become wiser and reflect on the need for change.

Dialogue is a fundamental way of communicating in a social system. It is a link between the individual consciousness and the social structure especially in large groups. Dialogue is different from discussion – with the purpose to convince – and from debate – with the purpose to win ('bat' them). In dialogue there is space and time for everyone to participate, learn, sense thoughts and feelings in the room. The outcome can be individual feedback to the participants and a shared view of what the participants think and want. The dialogue can result in common decisions and change.

The common insights and decisions become content and structure of the group culture. The British psychotherapist Pat de Maré expressed this in a simple formula:

*collective unconscious + dialogue --> collective conscious + culture*

When I have become conscious and when I have processed what I am conscious of, it is time to send my conclusions back to the unconscious and let my behavior be controlled from there. The equation also applies to groups, organizations and other social systems. This is how our basic assumptions from early childhood influence how we behave and react emotionally in present time. It is also through these processes that we can make our assumptions conscious and reconsider them.

## 5.2    Relating to Nature and Society

Inspired by Thomas Sowell's *A Conflict of Visions,* Steven Pinker describes in his book *The Blank Slate* two alternative visions for human development: the utopian and the tragic. In the utopian vision people can realize their dreams. Psychological obstacles and social arrangements cannot prevent us from heading towards a better world. In the tragic vision the human nature remains the same. The society subsists by developing strategies and laws to handle human egoism and human cruelties. From his own experience, Pinker estimates that 50% of the research results support the utopian vision and the other 50% the tragic vision.

There seem to be forces in nature and society acting in two directions: plus and minus, north and south, order and chaos. On the one hand, laws of nature might apply also in human and social contexts. On the other hand, it might be the human way of structuring the world. Philosophers refer to external reality and to our internal image of reality – the objective versus the subjective.

What are we actually becoming conscious of? To what

are we relating? – to an objective reality outside or to our internal image? Since there is no unifying conclusion, we seem to be stuck with this dialectic and the constant diversity of perspectives.

A human being is created from a few cells. In our lifetime, the cells differentiate and multiply into a complex system with a multitude of functions. After death, the cells disintegrate into a few chemical compounds. The work done by the individual in lifetime seems to be to keep the biological functions for the purpose of survival and of making the individual unique within the species. The life of the human being represents a movement counter to the striving of nature towards leveling and standardization.

Another aspect of nature is the continuously increasing degree of disorder. In the thermodynamic language: *entropy* always increases in a closed system. On a temporary basis, this can be prevented, by adding work to the system. Warm and cold become lukewarm, unless we provide work to keep the warm and cold apart. In a community, the mix of different kinds of people can be subject to the corresponding type of leveling. Powers in the society act to counteract this leveling and to preserve order. They can be destructive powers supporting segregation and ethnical rinsing. They can be good and constructive powers working for a clean, human and beautiful society.

From these perspectives on the human roles and options in nature and society, I will approach the question of *how to relate to what we are becoming conscious of* – individually and collectively.

## 5.3    Meaning, Trust and Power

Meaning, trust and power are three parallel aspects of a social context. I will here use them as guidelines for my interpretations and suggestions. These criteria can be related to the key words for leading: think, relate and influence. To be conscious of these guidelines and relate to them helps me to make decisions. The guidelines are mutually dependent on each other. It is not enough to think wisely – unless I also enjoy the power and the trust needed to implement my thoughts. If I have destructive thoughts and intentions, the combination of power and high trust can lead to unwanted consequences.

Below I will connect meaning to understanding and interpreting, trust to deepening and becoming wiser, power to changing and influencing.

### Meaning

The philosopher Immanuel Kant concluded that the human being has a fundamental need for meaning. He defined four categories: substance, time, space and cause-effect. Meaning and communication is possible only when we can relate to one or more of these categories.

Impressions from outside meet and are related to images already stored in the brain. They will be interpreted as identical or different. New images are stored in memory. This process shapes the fundamentals for thinking, language and meaning.

The language is actually based on images. Each word can normally be connected to a concrete image – a metaphor. Our images are converted to words and shape a meaningful context. Communication is about transferring and negotiating meaning between sender and receiver. The words carry the meaning. As was mentioned, the word 'dialogue' means 'through words' and indicates that a flow of words imply meaning.

It is a human privilege to be able to reflect on why, what and how before doing something. Aristotle used the concept *phronesis*, wisdom in action, for this option. To act wisely stands for thinking ethically and doing what I think is good and right. Ethical thinking includes reflecting on future actions – making myself conscious of reasons, motives, purposes and intentions behind what I am about to do. On the unconscious level, there are always ethical considerations or norms behind my actions. As well individually as in a social system, it is worthwhile to investigate the values mirrored in my actions and to discuss the ethical principles one wants to stand up for.

**Trust**

In all processes of exchange between people, we need to perceive that we can trust each other. The process often starts with a commitment – a deal of giving and receiving. It can be a business transaction, a marriage or a game. The need for confidence and trust depends on the situation and can vary from person to person. What do we mean by trust? Is it something that we can analyze intellectually or is it a straightforward emotional experience. I will treat confidence and trust as synonymous. Possibly trust represents a more overarching and long-range aspect of confidence.

Stephen M R Covey describes four *Cores of Trust*: *Integrity, Intention, Capability and Result*. Integrity stands for the extent to which a behavior corresponds to values expressed. Intention connotes whether the intention is open or hidden and also the ethics behind the action – good or evil intentions. Covey uses the notion of *Character* to represent integrity and intention. The notion of *Capability* refers to the ability to fix things. *Result* stands for the observed and measurable facts of what has been achieved. The notion of *Competence* refers to capability and result.

Trust is established over time and through various links. It starts with trust in myself – self-confidence. Probably, I cannot trust others unless I trust myself. In the same way as high self-esteem helps me appreciate others, self-confidence helps me trust others. Trust in interpersonal relations is the basis for trust in our social systems – trust within and in an organization, trust within and in the market, trust between suppliers and clients, trust within society.

Honesty and openness are two basic pillars for building trust. Honesty stands for my intention and drive to make my truth conscious to myself and others. Openness refers to my intention and drive to communicate my thoughts and feelings to others. These definitions leads to the conclusion that the less conscious I am of my own truth, the more distorted my open communication will be – and vice verse.

Truth is also an important aspect. However, truth is a problematic and difficult concept. Is there an objective truth – independent of human beings. Is truth completely subjective? Martin Buber differentiates between truth in three different contexts: the truth in court, the truth I tell others and the truth according to my conscience. The last one is the interpretation of truth I will stick to – 'my truth'.

Honesty begins with me being true to myself. This means striving to make myself conscious of my impressions and experiences, look at my images as they are. It also means being open to the feelings of joy and discomfort that might arise. As we have seen, I might unconsciously screen my truth off or consciously decide to do so. Just experiencing discomfort might be a reason enough for going a little deeper in order to explore my own truth. Strong feelings of discomfort are warning signals. My personal position is that honesty towards myself is an unconditional and absolute requirement. I think that it is valuable to be in touch with my own truth and to be open to myself. However, this internal openness depends on the situation. Feelings can sometimes be so strong that I consciously choose to withhold them. Temporarily, this can be quite a legitimate self-defense. However, strong feelings are often signals that there is something I need to confront.

I can choose what I am open with. To share my perceptions with others may lead to unwanted consequences and therefore I choose not to be open. However, I should be aware of my fear to tell something of which I am conscious. My fear for the consequences of being totally honest and open could make me withhold or even lie to others – and also to myself. To withhold in an important context could actually be a way of lying. In this situation, I think it is important to reflect on a deeper level on how to handle my fears. I also need to consider my task in this situation. Fear based upon (now) irrelevant basic assumptions may have fatal consequences for a current situation and for which I am responsible.

To build trust in relations is complex and demanding. All parties have to contribute by being honest and open. Everyone always has the opportunity to seek and explore one's own truth. Sometimes this exploration can be very challenging. We tend to trust people who are in touch with their feelings and accept the challenge.

## Power

*'A living being wants above all else to release its strength; life itself is the will to power'*
Friedrich Nietzsche

Friedrich Nietzsche claimed that the will to power is the main driving force in humans. He confirms the experience that power issues are essential and need to be taken into account in all social contexts.

Distance – or nearness – to power is one out of four factors that Geert Hofstede defines in his analysis of organization cultures. *Power distance* stands for to what extent people expect and accept that power is unevenly distributed. In cultures in which people are close to power, democratic and consultative attitudes are expected. Cultures with wide power distance are authoritative and paternalistic.

According to the FIRO theory the will to control is different from person to person and also the will to be controlled by others. The attitude to power in society mirrors the needs to control and to be controlled. Power is shaped in the meeting between individuals and culture, in groups and organizations. The power culture sets the conditions for co-operation and leading.

In a well functioning leading process the power issue has been resolved in a satisfactory way – for all parties. The leaders have taken the responsibility to make sure that the different parties have formal rights, means of control and feelings of freedom – criteria for to what extent the organization can meet its goals and visions.

## 5.4    Theories

Scientists, philosophers and other professional thinkers can help us understand and get answers to our questions on the issues we have become conscious of. Science does not give us univocal answers, rather hypotheses and theories to be tested. Theories are tracks of thought which we can use to interpret and explain what we encounter, speculate in possible future consequences and discuss necessary changes. Theories – scientific or not – support the decision process. At the end, I am as an individual the one to interpret and make my decisions.

To understand means different things:

- to explain how different events are connected
- to judge something based on current values: right/wrong, good/bad, wanted/not wanted
- to predict what is going to happen

Jon Elster suggests three types of explanations:

- Causal – what causes the event?
- Functional – what actual effects does the event have?
- Intentional – what is the intention behind what happens?

These ideas reconnect to the aforementioned perspectives on consciousness – the physical/biological, the psychological and the social. The causal and functional explanations are relevant in all the three perspectives, the intentional only in the psychological and social. I disregard how religion and mysticism sometimes explain physical and biological phenomena.

Assumptions about how it functions – a theory – shape the basis for understanding. The correctness of a scientific theory has been tested through observations. The scholarliness of a theory is sometimes important. For the purpose here, it is more important to get a starting point for interpretation and discourse – conversations which can give rise to better understanding, new questions and assumptions and new theories.

The theories that I will present below have this function. They have helped me understand human behavior as well as dynamics in groups and organizations.

The aforementioned **FIRO** theory about interpersonal relating is presented in detail in Appendix 3. It is useful in psychological and social contexts and primarily for understanding individual behavior on the group arena.

The three dimensions – inclusion, control and openness – correlate with the criteria mentioned above: meaning, power and trust. The connections power-control and trust-openness are unambiguous. Meaning stands for inclusion, in the sense that you have to include an idea in your agenda in order to consider it meaningful or not.

In the FIRO theory, I can interpret my behavior and my perceptions in meetings with others and myself. As stated earlier, these behaviors and perceptions are often unconscious and have roots in earlier assumptions in life. The extreme end positions oft he dimensions can be described as follows:

I am completely insignificant  <>  I am very significant
I am totally incompetent        <>  I am very competent
I am not likable at all          <>  I am very likable

Being outside the comfort zone and close to the extremes can result in irrelevant behaviors, exaggerations and understatements – too much or too little. If I perceive myself as not included in a satisfactory way, I can choose to stay out of the group completely or try to make myself appear as a very important person. If I do not like the way others try to control me, I can let things just be (*laissez-faire*) or choose to take the lead and totally control the situation myself. If I feel a person is coming too close and being too open to me, I can choose to completely close myself or tell the person almost everything that is on my mind.

My personal experience and belief is that comfort zones set in my childhood can be reconsidered and changed. In every moment, I can think that I have chosen to be in a certain way up to now. I can choose to adopt and learn another way to act from now on. When I have become aware of my behavior and have an emotional contact with the underlying assumptions, I have more self-insight and concrete experience to relate to. This is when self-acceptance and self-esteem become important aspects of my way of being. On the one hand, I need to accept and appreciate myself for what I have been up to now – in order to question, reconsider and move my boundaries without loosing self-esteem. On the other hand, I can recognize when my self-esteem is being threatened and what I tend to do when being outside my comfort zone. I also understand that changing myself requires patience and caring for myself.

There is a need for support in the individual process of change. In the following I will describe a model that has helped me understand personal and social change processes on a deeper level.

**The Four Rooms of Change** (*Förändringens Fyra Rum*®) is a theory of change. It assumes that there are four different psychological states representing four different ways of relating to the unconscious. Claes Janssen, the founder of the theory, describes the states in terms of behaviors and feelings as follows:

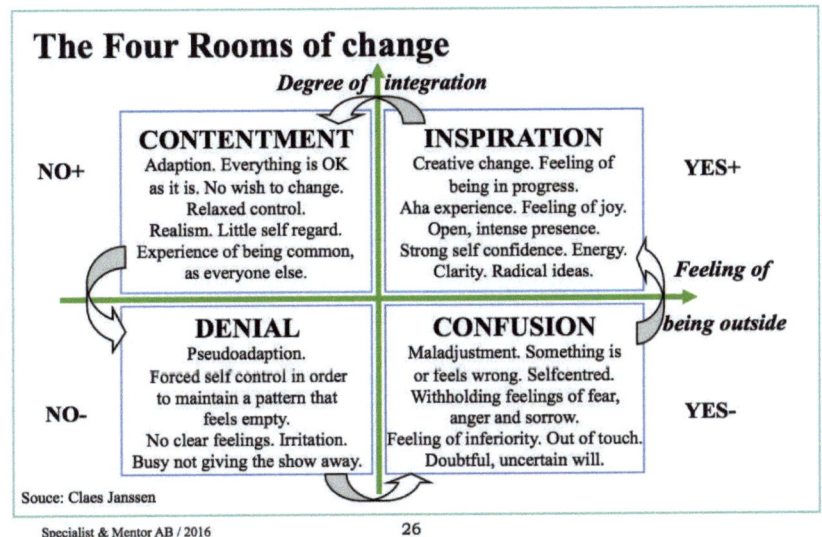

The Four Rooms of change
Degree of integration

CONTENTMENT
NO+
Adaption. Everything is OK as it is. No wish to change. Relaxed control. Realism. Little self regard. Experience of being common, as everyone else.

INSPIRATION
YES+
Creative change. Feeling of being in progress. Aha experience. Feeling of joy. Open, intense presence. Strong self confidence. Energy. Clarity. Radical ideas.

Feeling of

DENIAL
Pseudoadaption. Forced self control in order to maintain a pattern that feels empty. No clear feelings. Irritation. Busy not giving the show away.
NO-

CONFUSION
Maladjustment. Something is or feels wrong. Selfcentred. Withholding feelings of fear, anger and sorrow. Feeling of inferiority. Out of touch. Doubtful, uncertain will.
YES-

being outside

Souce: Claes Janssen

Specialist & Mentor AB / 2016          26

Janssen suggests that we pass through the four rooms in a circular movement from one stage to the next, from denial to confusion, to inspiration, to contentment and back to denial and confusion. The time we spend in the different rooms may vary and we always have the choice to go on to the next room. Below I will describe a 'trip' through the four rooms.

I start in the **denial** room – a state in which I tend to screen myself off from something unpleasant – *I censor myself*. One reason might be an experience of chock, for instance an accident or a sudden death of a near one. It can also be an unconscious experience of slowly increasing discomfort. After some time in the denial room, something happens that makes me 'de-censor', become more aware of the situation and start talking more openly about my discomfort and its causes. It can be myself taking initiative or someone else confronting me. This can be the start of change pushing or pulling me into the **confusion** room. In the confusion room, my discomfort is conscious and I try to live with it. My challenge is to stand the discomfort and move on, passing what Janssen calls the 'zero point'. An alternative is to go back to the denial room. In the confusion room, I scrutinize myself, my self-concept, arrive at new insights that can result in a decision to move on. I enter the **inspiration** room, in which I have an enhanced feeling of happiness. Everything goes my way – perhaps an experience of *flow*. The unconscious experiences in this room can be unrealistic expectations of what is possible to achieve. To become aware of the realistic possibilities and wisely accept them leads to the fourth room, the **contentment** room. In this room, I can take it easy and 'harvest' the result of my efforts to change. The circle is completed and I have found a new state of balance. In this way my trip through life goes on via the four rooms.

The FIRO theory and the Four Rooms of Change put personal behavior in a psychological perspective and describes the underlying perceptions and feelings. Both theories give us clues to understanding human interaction in social systems – groups, teams and organizations – and change processes in these systems.

The climate in a social system can be mapped by using these theories. Also, in a social system one can talk about self-insight, self-acceptance and self-esteem as pre-requisites for change. In the FIRO theory, the climate can be described in terms of the behavior dimensions – inclusion, control and openness – and the perceptions of being significant, competent and likable. The result of a climate investigation can be interpreted as a collective comfort zone influenced by the individual comfort zones, the demands set by the mission and the management. The result also signals dissatisfaction with the current climate and with circumstances that are questioned and eventually should be changed. In the terms of the Four Rooms of Change theory, the climate and the readiness to change can be investigated with the Organization Barometer (*Organisationsbarometern®*). Too high levels of denial and confusion are warning signals as well as too low levels of inspiration and contentment. The barometer points at circumstances which require attention and eventually need to be changed.

The roles in a social system can be matched through the personal comfort zones as described in the FIRO theory. Persons being high in including and controlling others fit well together with persons who prefer to be included and controlled. In the same way, positions in the organizations can be described in terms of the FIRO dimensions and thus matched against the applicants' individual preferences.

Being outside my comfort zone challenges my flexibility, my capacity to temporarily adapt my behavior and over time change my comfort zone. Then, the last of my sample of theories might be useful.

**The Human Element** (THE) is primarily a pedagogical model. The aforementioned FIRO theory is the basis and has been complemented with more assumptions. Will Schutz calls them *"the human elements – per-*
*sonal fears, rigidities and defenses and all the other real reasons*
*why human events do not take place more smoothly in organiza-*
*tions"*. Schutz assumed that these human elements are
related to people's self-esteem. Low self-esteem in an
organization leads to turbulence, frustrations and mis-
directed actions. Human energy is used for defensiveness, withholding and other interpersonal struggles.
The capacity to learn is reduced. People are in conflict.
Productivity and efficiency drop.

Example 1:     Collaborators do not meet the demands
of their roles and tasks or are on the wrong job – having tasks that they are not qualified or prepared for.
Managers do not recognize this situation.

Example 2: The leaders lock themselves up in established patterns and do not recognize what the situation
and the organization demand.

The theoretical explanation of these behaviors is this:
People unconsciously defend themselves agains unpleasant feelings – for instance the fear of not coping,
not getting enough attention or being disliked – defenses based on low self-esteem.

THE raises the question on how one can understand
and influence the self-esteem of the individuals in a social system. My conclusion is that I, myself, am the only one who is in contact with my feelings of discomfort
and can take responsibility for my self-esteem. The

leaders can be models by continuously strengthening and learning to handle their own self-esteem. The leaders can lead by creating good circumstances – for instance learning situations – which make it possible and inspiring for collaborators to increase their self-insight, self-acceptance and self-esteem.


## 5.5   Wisdom

Through exploration, reflection and change, people and organizations get access to new knowledge and experiences that are added to the old ones and shape new layers for the consciousness to penetrate. Sedimented layers of earth and an unpeeled onion are two useful metaphors. You dig in the earth to make use of deeper layers or to hide things. The onion has many layers and as you get deeper into it, tears tend to come out of your eyes. To deepen your self-concept can be thought of as getting in touch with deeper layers inside yourself – the inner core. This process can be heavy and unpleasant. It can also be joyful and filled with new valuable discoveries.

People who have managed their way through painful experiences and periods in life often radiate wisdom. They might have learnt to be honest to the situation and open to their own experience. I cannot choose my accidents. I can choose my way to relate to them. By exploring new ways to confront difficulties and by reconsidering my basic assumptions, I can move on from difficult periods with new conclusions and more wisdom.

In a social context, there is a collective search for truth and common handling of events and developments. Just as for an individual, these search processes can be risky for an organization. It might not survive. In a global perspective, I think there is a need for taking risks and for turning organizations over. Some dissolve and others move on after having enhanced their collective wisdom.


## 5.6    Change

*It is not possible to change others. If you need to change others in order to satisfy yourself, you will never be content, because there is only one person that you could possibly change.*
Bertil Magnusson (in my translation)

A decision to change is eventually preceded by exploration and interpretation of the current situation. This decision process has both conscious and unconscious levels. Sometimes the decision process can be very conscious and last for a long period of time. In emergency situations, most of the exploration and the interpretation take place on an unconscious deep level in the lower parts of the brain.

Change can be related to two factors: 1) a situation – the consequence of a number of preceding events or actions – and 2) a driving force which changes the situation and makes the series of events take a new direction. The British anthropologist Gregory Bateson minted the expression *'a difference that makes a difference'*. As a metaphor he used a car that drives on a road with a bump. Approaching the bump in high speed (the driving force) means that the car changes direction, although only for a short while. With low speed the car passes the bump smoothly and continues in the same direction. The driving force has at least two components – a direction (a goal or a vision) and the power driving in the chosen direction.

The American management consultant Robert Fritz has developed a model for change based on three components: 1) current situation, 2) wanted situation and 3) plan of action. Behind each situation is an underlying structure of more or less hidden circumstances. Like the water flowing in a river passes stones and other obstacles, the flow of events evolves through the underlying structure of hidden history.

According to Fritz, the flow of events will oscillate back and forth between the current and the wanted situation unless the plan of action is firmly connected to both the wanted and the current situation. Real change needs to be structural and based on an intense experience of *tension* between the wanted and the current situation. For this purpose, the wanted and the current situation needs to be expressed in the same terms. An example:

CURRENT       Different energy sources are being used
SITUATION  – fossil, biological, water, sun and wind.

WANTED
SITUATION Only renewable energy sources are used.

The change from the current to the wanted situation requires certain *primary* decisions to be taken. In this energy example, political decisions are needed for driving the changes of production, distribution and consumption of energy.

The plan of action implements the primary decisions through a number of *secondary* decisions. Provided the plan of action identifies the primary decisions and is well anchored in the current and the wanted situations, the implementation will release the tension between the two situations.

Great and radical changes touch upon all the aforementioned perspectives – the physical-biological, the individual-psychological and the social. In each perspective, the structural obstacles are represented. Together they represent a complex challenge for those involved. To arrive at a shared vision and identify the primary decisions requires knowledge and insight.

The decision to change can be a big intellectual challenge. It can be compared with the problem of playing the Japanese game sudoku. In every square there are normally more than one alternative. If I choose one of the alternatives, the possibilities to find the right solution in the end might be locked. The trick is to be patient, wait, continue looking for alternatives and systematically identify the possible combinations.

There are tragic examples of decisions leading to unwanted consequences. The psychologist Manfred Kets de Vries points at the phenomenon of *folie à deux* – shared psychosis. A person with a strong delusional belief attracts others to support – in the worst case a whole nation. A well-known case is the cause of events in Germany lead by Hitler and his supporters. This example shows how a deeply anchored attitude to the current situation can lead to an insane vision (world supremacy and extinction of Jews) and an insane action plan.

How to change deeply anchored attitudes with a great number of people? This is a crucial question and a big challenge? However, the question is actually irrelevant rather than crucial. The only one who can change your attitude is you yourself. Assuming that we create our selves by relating to others, it is reasonable to assume that the social situation has influence on the members. Herbert C Kelman has in his research arrived at three fundamental ways of relating which people choose from when being challenged by external pressure to change their attitudes.

1) *Compliance* is chosen when pressure is exerted with undue means, for instance through physical or mental violence. Reluctantly, one assumes the wanted attitude and acts according to instructions – or the way one thinks is right according to the wanted attitude.

2) *Identification* is chosen when one accepts external influence because one wants a good relationship to those exerting the pressure. Perhaps they are perceived as important, competent ore caring.

3) *Internalization* is chosen when the external attitude is in line one's own values. The wanted attitude is perceived as immediately useful for solving one's own problems. It is therefore unproblematic to

assume this attitude and make it one's own.

These strategic alternatives connect to the aforementioned criteria power, trust and meaning. Compliance is a reasonable choice when subject to power. Identification is a sign of trusting those exerting power. Internalizing is the choice when the wanted attitude has a deeper meaning.

Integration is often an ultimate goal in all types of change in complex contexts. All those involved have integrated attitudes, values and behaviors. On the one hand, this means that the different parts of a chosen strategy are connected and contribute to the wanted development. On the other hand, integration means that attitudes and behaviors are fully accepted and to a great extent unconscious.

## 5.7    Pause for Reflection

Below I will present a method to achieve an inner dialogue in order to get in touch with my inner core. It is
a way of thinking in which I can guide myself or ask
someone else to guide me. The method is included in
The Human Element seminar. The primary purpose is
to invite you to reflect on the method itself. If you
want to apply it right now, make sure that you have
plenty of time and that you are in a secure environment – alone or together with people you trust. It is
important for all involved to have good intentions, to
be mentally and physically present, to understand the
context and to care for each other.

Since the inner core can hide personal problems, cause
loss of energy and prevent productive work, it can be
essential to be in touch with the inner core. Approaching the inner core should be respectful and caring, respecting the inner forces. It is only you, yourself, who
has the right to approach your inner core. It can be
recommended and supported by someone else, but it is
you, yourself, who asks for support in the guiding and
in the analysis. Remember that you have a valuable inner power in your inner core. It can be threatening and
frightening, especially if it is let out too quickly or at
the wrong moment.

This is how you do the experiment. I recommend that
you do this thought experiment in a rather high tempo
– about 30 seconds for each step.

1) Close your eyes, take a deep breath and relax.
2) Think of three characteristics of yourself, the ones you like best about yourself. Imagine you have these three characteristics. Be aware of your feeling.
3) Rank these characteristics from 1 to 3, 1 being the most important.
4) Imagine yourself having 1and 2, but not 3. Be aware of your feeling.
5) Imagine having 1, but not 2 or 3. Be aware of your feeling.
6) Imagine yourself having none of these three characteristics. Be aware of your feeling.

   Perhaps you feel discomfort without the good characteristics you have chosen. There could also be something behind these characteristics that you don't like.

7) If you don't like what you experience – or if you would like to change it – try to see if you can change the image of yourself into something you want. Decide what you want and imagine your image of yourself being changed.

8) If you find this difficult, picture a friend or a wise person you know, who could help you change the image of yourself into something you like better.

If you do not arrive at a joyful experience, you have demonstrated for yourself that there might be something unpleasant within you that you eventually should explore. This might take more time. Then, it is especially important that you allow yourself that time and that you give yourself patience and compassion.

Through this exercise you can increase your self-esteem. In the contact with you inner layers, you can discover aspects of yourself that you were not aware of. They could be aspects of yourself that you don' t want to see. They can also be qualities that you wished you had – and now you can reach and enhance them.

# 6 PHRONESIS

## 6.1 The Mission

*The responsibility is that of the individual who will rely neither on a form of power nor on a god. You must engage – your humanity demands it.*
Stéphane Hessel

It is time to return to the context presented in the beginning of this book – the mission for humanity to ensure survival of the species and to maintain a sustainable society. My assumption is that the long-range development of nature and society is controlled from underlying structures. Continuously increasing disorder – entropy – is one of the laws of nature. The direction is fixed. The pace is influenced by the underlying structures. I think the challenge for humanity is to balance on 'waves' towards total disorder by wisely and skillfully explore, understand and change established structures – and to create new ones.

The aforementioned notion of *phronesis* signifies the quality of action, how something is done and the intention behind the action. According to José Luis Ramìrez one can interpret the ethics of Aristotle as *action ethics*. Good actions shape the foundation for good production and good products. Aristotle made a useful distinction between acting (*praxis*), doing (*poiesis*) and the result (*factum*). An action is characterized by the quality of the intention – more or less good. The doing can be performed with more or less skills. The result can be evaluated against the intentions. Me writing this book is what I do, the thoughts behind represent my action and the printed book is the result of my work.

I think that we need clear and shared visions for the future in order to reach wanted results – visions which can be picked up by people's thoughts and feelings and which give directions for how good intentions can be converted to skillful performance and wanted results.

A current vision is a sustainable society. The concept of sustainability needs to be interpreted and converted into sub-visions that are directed towards different groups in society. How are the conditions on Earth when the population development is stabilized and under control? How can the sub-vision 'clean water for all' be converted into concrete commitments and measures? Do we want a society based on 100% renewable energy sources to be more global or more dependent upon local supply?

Agreements and commitments are foundations for the functioning of organizations and the society. In the global community, leaders, experts, politicians and administrators strive to reach agreements on shared visions and commitments to action plans.

Current examples are the *Global Development Goals* (GDG:s) and the climate agreements. The 17 GDG:s were in 2015 accepted by most of the nation states and form the basis for action plans under the *2030 Agenda*. GDG no 13 states:

*Take urgent action to combat climate change and its impacts – Acknowledging that the United Nations Framework Convention on Climate Change is the primary international, intergov-*

*ernmental forum for negotiating the global response to climate change.*

After many rounds and ups-and-downs of climate negotiations the global community reached an agreement i Paris in December 2015. The participating nation states agreed to

*holding the increase in the global average temperature to well below 2 °C above pre-industrial levels and pursuing efforts to limit the temperature increase to 1.5 °C.*

These examples illustrate the difficulty that Robert Fritz points at – the anchoring of the plan of action to the current and the wanted situation. The current climate situation is being questioned and debated. How to measure the average global temperature? To what extent do we humans cause the greenhouse effect? The wanted situation is not straightforward and subject to compromises. It is still (in July 2017) not clear whether all nation states will commit to the Paris agreement. The action plan does not yet release the tension between the current and the wanted situation.

## 6.2   The Will

*All human beings are born free and equal in dignity and rights. They are endowed with reason and conscience and should act towards one another in a spirit of brotherhood.*
The Universal Declaration of Human Rights

Whether the will is free or not is a philosophical question which science cannot – yet – give an answer to.

Since we do not have scientifically and generally established conclusions, it is reasonable to assume that everyone has a say. The question of free will is also a moral issue: to what extent do I think that I am responsible for my actions?

Statements about free will oscillate between the philosophical extremes: determinism and indeterminism. From a determinism standpoint, everything has a cause. Every event is preceded and explained by another event. The noble prize award Francis Crick held that everything we do has a scientific explanation – physical, chemical, neurological or other. This statement might be perceived as frightening. Some of us like to think that we can influence the process, at least to some extent.

Will Schutz suggested another way to relate to free will – in the atmosphere of American pragmatism: Imagine you choose everything. Is this thought useful? Which are the consequences of assuming free will? Are there accidents? – or just bad choices? Is my stress caused by external factors? Can I choose to avoid stress? These questions invite me to go back and reflect on my conclusions. I am also invited to consider changing the situation by changing my behavior.

My own conclusion is that I choose my way to relate to what happens. Sometimes it happens very quickly and I have almost no time to think. Then, my choice is unconscious. It could be an innate behavior taking over, like fleeing from a sudden threat. It could also be a learned behavior based on similar situations and choices earlier in life. In every situation, I am responsible for my unconscious and conscious contributions and the consequences.

The assumption of free will means that every human being has personal freedom. Everyone can make one's own choices and take responsibility for one's own life. Personal freedom is the fundamental human right that has been confirmed in international conventions, for instance The Universal Declaration of Human Rights in 1948 and The European Convention in 1950. The UN declaration states that every human being has been equipped with wit and conscience to act towards each other in an atmosphere of brotherhood. This means personal responsibility in relating to others in all social contexts.

## 6.3    The Social Context

When I think of humanity as a species and a sustainable community, I imagine that all humans in some way are connected in a global social web. In this 'global theory', all humans on earth are included in a common social context – *the global community*. However, I also think that most activities and operations in the world tend to limit this perspective to a social context that can be controlled. I will give an example.

The international standard ISO 26000 for social responsibility, adopted in 2010, is an attempt to control sustainability. It addresses stakeholders within an organization's 'sphere of influence'. Stakeholders are individuals, groups and organizations whose needs and interests can influence and be influenced by the operations. The influence is exerted on humans and environment, economy and society.

Identifying the stakeholders of an operation means to position the operation in a social context. From influence on operations follows that people need to be in touch and relate to each other in order to map and estimate the effects of the influence. They also need to agree on necessary attitudes and measures.

The stakeholders of an organization can be divided in the following five categories:

- Clients, members and other users

- Suppliers, subcontractors and partners

- Employees and others active in the organization, like hired personnel

- Owners

- Community – local and global, media, citizens and other individuals connected tot he community

Stakeholders belong to the social operations system, in which everyone depends upon everyone according to the global theory. The system can be represented as a circle on which all stakeholders are related to the organization and to each other. The interests can be legal, environmental, economic and human. An interest can concern one stakeholder or more.

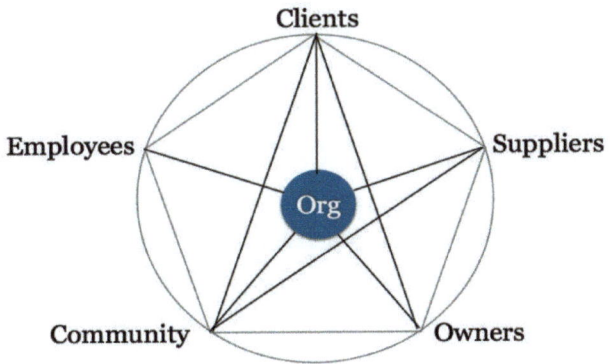

Involving the stakeholders, means having a dialogue with all of them exploring the needs, interests and dependencies. The purpose of this dialogue is to map the conditions and establish trust for co-operation in the operations system and for handling conflicts of interest. The notions of meaning, power and trust can be developed into concrete criteria for evaluating the conditions for co-operation with and between the stakeholders.

## 6.4 The Responsibility

*You are responsible as individuals*
Jean-Paul Sartre

Individual responsibility is the foundation for responsibility in organizations and in the community. Collective choices and decisions can always be referred to the choice made by individuals. This is being clearly addressed by Wilhelm Röpke in his analysis before the political election in Germany in 1930:

*No one who votes for the National Socialists on September 14 should be able to say he did not know what might come out of it. He should know that he is voting for chaos in place of order, destruction in the place of reconstruction. He should know that he is voting for war at home and senseless destruction abroad. Vote, but vote in a way such that you will not feel any complicity in the catastrophe that may yet erupt upon us.*

The idea of collective responsibility follows from regarding the group as an individual subject. From inside and outside, the group is looked upon as a unit – 'one for all, all for one'. This could be an agreement that all the members have committed themselves to follow. Still, assuming free will there is always a possibility to break the loyalty, eventually followed by penalty. If the group disorganizes, the individual responsibilities for the collective actions remain. Normally, the formal responsibility of the group is delegated to the leader – the CEO or the chairman of the board. Thus, the collective responsibility is always subordinated the individual.

This is not my table' meaning ,this is not my responsibility' is a common statements. It delimits and focuses in such a way that the world outside can be ignored. However, it is important to listen to signals from the outside world and to reconsider the established demarcations. This is also a part of the responsibility – the individual as well as the collective.

## 6.5 Social Responsibility and Sustainable Development

Social Responsibility (SR) is an attitude aiming at confronting the global challenges and contributing to sustainable development (SD). In 2010, the aforementioned international standard ISO 26000 was adopted, with the intention to support SR and SD. It is called a 'guiding standard'. This means that organizations cannot get certified. They have to show in action that they apply the seven principles of the standard.

According to ISO 26000 SR stands for:
*the responsibility of an organization for the impact of its decisions and activities on society and the environment, through transparent and ethical behavior which*

- *contributes to sustainable development, including health and the welfare of society;*
- *takes into account the expectations of stakeholders;*
- *is in compliance with applicable law and consistent with international norms of behavior;*
- *is integrated throughout the organization and practiced in its relationships*

The seven principles are

:

1) *Accountability* – be responsible, accept control, prevent repetition
2) *Transparency* – make public, be clear and understandable
3) *Ethical behavior* – values and principles, especially in the absence of laws
4) *Respect for stakeholder interests* – identify, acknowledge

5) *Respect for the rule of law* – accept obligations, keep informed
6) *Respect for international norms of behavior* – moral in the absence of laws
7) *Respect for human rights* – acknowledge, apply, promote

to be integrated in two main objectives:

I *Identify and involve stakeholders within the sphere of influence*
II *Apply social responsibility in relevant areas of operation*

There are practical problems implementing SR in society. The organizations are expected to take responsibility for their own operations and economy. At the same time they are required to look for possibilities to improve their economy by involving other areas of responsibility. ISO 26000 aims at changing attitudes and behaviors in organizations. The integrations process is crucial when it comes to collective and individual responsibility. In spite of thorough argumentation and systematic pedagogics, the basic question remains: How to make SR and SD profitable, to provide revenues, not only costs?

To integrate an idea from outside into an organization stands for making the idea conceived as self-evident by everyone involved. To make this internal motivation active in meetings and dialogues with the stakeholders also requires external changes. In order to have organizations integrate SR, respecting all stakeholders in the sphere of influence has to be generally accepted as well inside the organization as by the outside community.

External motivation is supported by the definitions of SR: care for the environment, enhance human health and contribute to SD. This external motivation works well in some contexts and less well in others. In the non-profit sector, these ideas have since long time ago been established and strongly integrated. In the public sector there is a traditional difference in attitude between the left and the right politics. This polarization is slowly changing with the appearance of new parties and with sustainability being on the political agenda. In the business sector, companies more and more connect SR to the external motivation – brand, customer loyalty, recruiting, respect for local laws and prescriptions – and regard these motivations as critical conditions for the survival and profitability of the company.

The requirements for SR on a collective level are to some extent met in our society. Quite a number of institutions and organizations show that they are ready and motivated to take responsibility for environment and people in the sphere of influence. In order to make these attitudes sustainable, the leaders and the collaborators need to integrate the external declarations on a deeper level. A sustainable society is dependent on individuals taking responsibility – and also on the established systems and structures in organizations and communities. Thus, SR and SD ask for change initiatives from the leaders and the collaborators as well as in the systems and routines.

## 6.6    Values and Ethics

One problem with sustainability is the long-term perspective. Many of our systems in society, such as market economy, free competition and tax systems drive towards short-range planning and acting. Unprofitable operations are not accepted by these systems – at least not on a long-range basis. Long-term decisions normally require sacrifices, such as investments and unpaid personal time. Big social investments, for example in infrastructure, often require political interventions through laws and regulations. This is where ethical standpoints come into the picture. Ethical beliefs can be reflected in the values, practices and policies, which shape the choices made by decision makers on behalf of their organizations. A long-range perspective needs ethics. However, ethics is often thought of as causing extra costs and deteriorating profitability. Therefore, ethics needs to be evaluated also from an economic point of view. In analogy with culture, ecological products and sports it ought to be possible to attach economic value also to ethics. Organizations, which invest in the implementation and the application of ethical value systems, could charge the clients and get tax reductions.

Creating sustainable nature and a sustainable human society indicates a commitment to ethical values. To promote actions which I value as good and right is exactly the purpose of ethics. Like the concepts of reality, consciousness and free will, ethics is a philosophical issue. *Meta-ethics* or value theory is a philosophical discipline studying ethics as a phenomenon. Can ethics be objective and transferred from generation to generation or is ethics subjective and only connected to the person who stands up for it? *Normative ethics* is concerned with directives for what is to be regarded as acceptable ethical values.

In this context, I will focus on *applied ethics*. Applied ethics stands for my way of being ethical in general and for how I practice my personal ethics in specific situations. This is clearly *subjective* – what I consider to be good and right. To apply ethics in practice means to reflect and decide on what I consider good and right in general and in specific situations. The steps could be as follows:

1) make myself conscious of circumstances which has an effect on or are affected by my operations - and to be open to myself about it

2) reflect on what I am conscious of, understand, change (if needed) and deepen

3) discuss with others and get their feedback

4) decide, make a personal choice

5) act according to my decision

It is especially important to recognize my feelings arising from my observations and thoughts. These feelings signal that my ethics might need to be reflected on. As has been mentioned earlier, our feelings are sometimes so strong and awful that we prefer to defend ourselves against them. This can be perfectly legitimate when it is clear that the cause of my feelings is out of my personal influence and control. However, when I perceive that I could have done something or could do it differently, it is time for applied ethics.


## 6.7 Code of Action

By 'code of action' (CoA) I mean a set of behavioral rules which the leaders and the collaborators commit themselves to apply. The CoA expresses the organization's applied ethics, internal prescriptions for good and right actions. CoA also represents the expectations that the collaborators have on each other regarding professional, efficient and sustainable behavior.

CoA needs to be integrated into the whole organization and thus being the basis for all current activities. This is especially important in unpredicted and emergency situations. The organization's way of acting in such situations shows to what extent the ethics expressed also is the ethics applied – if Code of Action is *Code in Action*.

CoA represents a sustainable attitude to be adopted by generations of leaders and collaborators. However, CoA also has to be questioned and developed. When long-term and complex decisions are at stake, there should be time for reflection – time to reconsider CoA in relation to new knowledge and technology, new and anticipated laws and prescriptions.

By having and applying a CoA, organizations can build trust in its network of stakeholders, 'strengthen and position the brand' as a brand strategist would express it. Establishing a code of action as an ethical attitude in the underlying structure creates trust for the organization and the whole operations system. An example is the aforementioned development of the gastric ulcers medicine Losec.

CoA can also support the systematic application of social responsibility in an organization. ISO 26000 offers a structure for the content of CoA. The seven principles are applied to each group of stakeholders for the purpose of finding, which rules of action apply to the different principles. The behaviors suggested mirror the values. These external values need to be correlated with the organization's current internal values. The leaders and the collaborators can also be invited to correlate with their personal values. This work process could result in revisions of the different values and in an operative CoA.

## 6.8  In Search of the Leading Self

Applying CoA – in other words CiA, *Code in Action* – is an example of how *phronesis* can work in practice. Creating as well as applying CoA requires wise action and skillful performance. The leaders need to co-operate with the organization and make use of the collaborators' competence. There is also a need for well functioning routines and continuous improvement everywhere in the organization.

Wise leading is not a question of behavioral rules in the CoA, rather about the leaders' attitude and ways to relate to the flow of events. This was in the first chapter connoted *dynamic leadership* – capacity to handle current deviations here and now. In the wise organization, there is continuous learning. Behavioral norms are introduced early in the learning process. In the long-term, these learnings are adopted as intuitive behaviors.

In this book, focus has been on the learning process, learning for everyone in the organization. The leader can be a model in this learning process. The leaders need capacity to access their self-insight and to take responsibility for their self-esteem in order to inspire the collaborators to develop these capacities on their own. In this way, both the leader and the collaborators can build their platforms for wise action as well towards the clients and suppliers as internally towards each other. The leader is the director. This is how I would like to summarize the key words of the leader's repertoire:

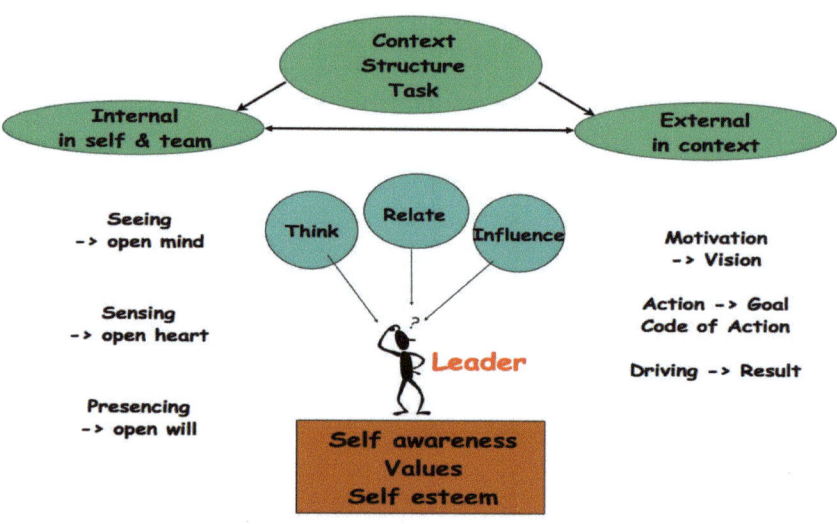

The mission is the survival of humans as a species on Earth. How can the individual leading processes contribute? Perhaps is it like in the aforementioned example of the crew being on the ship in a storm – 'all hands on deck': one hand is needed for staying on the boat and the other hand for securing the continuation of the journey.

There is a need for leading self all the way from the individual via our organizations to the global community. I have come to the conclusion that the appropriate leading processes need leaders who wisely handle their life experience and collaborators who together with the leaders work from inside out based on self-insight and self-esteem. The organization can be regarded as a copy of the human organism. There are potentials in our organizations, like there is potential in each of us. In the same way as the *me* can learn to function in the team, the *organization* can learn to function in the local and global communities.

The learning processes on the higher organization levels are very much slower and more inefficient than on the lower and more individual levels. This means that finding and delivering the potentials on the higher levels take more time. The need for better leading processes on national and global levels is obvious. The search for leading selves for the global tasks needs to be promoted. The climate situation indicates that there is no time to lose. Hopefully it goes faster when more of us see our own potentials and are inspired to take part in the leading processes – and in the search for our own leading self.

# EPILOGUE

*He* (Zhuangzi, c 369 - 286 BC) *would say that we should think of creativity as emerging when we move beyond the confines of a single great 'self' and open ourselves up to a larger cosmos.*
Michael Puett & Christine Gross-Loh

*I think that consciousness is the way information feels when being processed in certain complex ways, and that the particular kind of consciousness that we humans subjectively perceive arises when your brain's model of you is interacting with your brain's model of the world.*
Max Tegmark

The content of the original book, *Ledning sökes,* was designed in 2010-11. In this book, the content has been redrafted and elucidated – and updated to what I perceive as the current situation in 2017.

Especially, these things have happened in the meantime:

- The global climate negotiations took a significant step forward through the agreement in Paris in December 2015.

- The consulting group, 4F, that in 2012 published the book *Ledning sökes* has wound up.

- I have written another book – published in 2017: *Beyond Self - Ways of Thinking in Complex Environments*

In the meantime, I have learnt to appreciate many more perspectives on the idea of leading self – and to integrate my understanding of self with insights from my basic training in science, mathematics and physics. By going 'beyond self' I mean searching backwards and forwards in time, outwards in space and deeper inwards. Exploring 'beyond self' is actually a key to self-awareness. Going backwards in time and outwards in space have given me new perspectives on as well leadership as sustainability.

It has, for example, been an enriching experience to read *The Path* by the professor Michael Puett and the journalist Christine Gross-Loh. They state that the modern emphasis on the individual and the self has roots in the Protestant and Calvinistic movements in the 16th century. Already the Chinese philosophers, long before Christ, recognized that our emotions and instincts take over in complex situations and that we humans actually stand in our own way. Searching within ourselves might actually limit us. Our ability to handle emotions and self rather develops by looking outward.

I have also got inspiration from *Our Mathematical Universe* by Max Tegmark. In Tegmark's mathematical universe the human being consists of roughly $10^{29}$ elementary particles and the human life is described as patterns in the four dimensions of space-time. Our awareness of time and space is our inner model of the external reality made up in our brains. There might even be an infinite number of copies of us out there, which all experience the world in the same ways as we do. Our 'unique' identity exists only in our internal reality. Our perceptions of self and time are illusions.

The Chinese concept of *Dao*, the Way, and Tegmark's mathematical model of the universe give rise to two very different ways of interpreting the future. One stands for a lot of potential choices, the other for no choice at all.

On the Way, we continually shape our future through our daily thoughts, choices and actions. I recall what I sometimes reflected as a child: what has happened up to now can be left behind and I can always start on a very different track from now on. In every moment, I can change my way of being. As a sustainable human being I continuously follow and react to the daily events in my life.

In the space-time model, my future is like a DVD that I have not yet seen the end of. My future is that sample of all possible future impressions that match my current observations and in the patterns which define my space-time existence. Sustainability is built into the DVD and is a consequence of the stability of the mathematical laws.

With reference to these very different models of reality, I invite you to try them both, reflect upon your own way of thinking and leading – up to now and from now on – and to anticipate emerging futures – your own and others'.

# APPENDICES

# APPENDIX 1: GLOSSARY

| Concept | Comment | Section |
|---|---|---|
| Altruism | Unselfishness, concern for others, the opposite of egoism. | 1.3, 2.4, 3.1, 3.7 |
| Code of Action | The principles and rules which a person or an organization adopt and intend to apply when acting. | 6.7 |
| Collective unconsciousness | The notion of an inherent unconscious psyche, common for all human beings – introduced by Carl Gustav Jung (1875-1961). | 2.5, 3.4, 4.4-5, 5.1 |
| Comfort Zone | A repertoire of behaviors and emotions, which a person is comfortable with. | 1.3, 1.6, 3.2-3, 3.7-8, 4.4-5, 5.4 |
| Consciousness | Here: a human being's knowledge about psychic phenomena within or in an outer context. | 2.3, 2.6, 4.1-4, 4.6, 5.1, 5.4-5, 6.6, Epilogue |

| Concept | Comment | Section |
|---|---|---|
| Defense mechanism | See Personal Defenses. | 1.5, 3.3, 4.3 |
| Dialogue | A format for communication – in a group or with oneself – including and heeding sensory impressions and thoughts as well as emotions. | Prologue, 1.5, 3.7, 4.5-6, 5.1, 5.3, 5.7, 6.3, 6.5 |
| DNA | Deoxyribonucleic acid, a molecule carrying genetic information for the development and functioning of the organism. | 3.5 |
| Ecological footprint | A measure of the average area that a human being uses for consumption, living, garbage disposals and all other needs. | 2.1 |
| Ego | The Ego actively co-ordinates the different parts of one's personality, relating to both the Self and the surrounding world, for example through the use of various defense mechanisms. See also Self and Personal defenses. | 1.3, 1.4 |

| Concept | Comment | Section |
|---|---|---|
| Egoism | Focus on oneself or one's own advantage, the opposite of altruism. | 1.2, 2.4, 3.1, 3.7, 5.2 |
| Ethics | The moral philosophy behind actions, whether they represent right or wrong, good or bad conduct. Also: a set of principles or rules of behavior. | 1.2, 1.4, 3.1, 4.2, 5.3, 6.1, 6.6-7 |
| Ethics, applied | A philosophical discipline dealing with how ethical norms are applied in real-life situations and concerning practical problems. | 1.2, 2.1, 6.6-7 |
| FIRO-theory | Fundamental Interpersonal Relations Orientation theory, a theory of human interactions developed by the American psychologist and scientist Will Schutz (1925–2002). | 1.3, 1.5, 3.2, 3.4, 3.8, 5.3-4, App 3 |

| Concept | Comment | Section |
|---------|---------|---------|
| Four Rooms of Change | A registered trademark and a psychological theory describing what happens to individuals, groups and organizations when undergoing change. The model was developed by the Swedish psychologist and scientist Claes F Janssen (1940– ). http://www.claesjanssen.com | 5.4 |
| Group Analysis | Methods for therapeutic work in groups, studying and facilitating the functioning of a group and the relations between group members. (see also Matrix) | 3.4, 3.5 |
| The Human Element® (THE) | A registered trademark and a training program with the aim of strengthening motivation, co-operation, leading and productivity within organizations – by guiding people to enhance self-awareness and responsibility for self-esteem. | Prokogue, 1.5, 1.7, 3.3, 5.4, 5.7 |

| Concept | Comment | Section |
|---|---|---|
| Human Rights | Universal rights applicable to all human beings in the world, af all nations and cultures – and thus in all social contexts. | Prologue, 2.5, 6.2, 6.5, App 3 |
| The Inner Core | A perceived composition of distinguishing traits which are thought of as hidden by surrounding layers of memories. The notion of the inner code can be applied to both individuals and organizations. | 4.3-4, 5.5, 5.7 |
| The Integral Model | A model including many different perspectives on physical and mental processes, developed by Ken Wilber (1949-) | 4.6-7 |
| Integration | The co-ordination or joining af parts in a whole, bringing together to unity. | 4.6, 5.6, 6.5 |

| Concept | Comment | Section |
| --- | --- | --- |
| Integrity | Adherence to moral and ethical principles. Sense of 'uncorrupted virtue' | 5.3 |
| Internalization | The process of incorporating others' thoughts, values and patterns of reaction – making them one's own. | 5.3 |
| ISO 26000 | An international standard intended to guide and assist organizations in social responsibility and contributing to sustainable development. It was adopted in 2010 by more than 90 countries. | 6.3, 6.5, 6.7 |
| Leadership | The role which leaders choose to take and perform. In this book personal leadership focuses on the leaders' ways of thinking, relating and affecting. | Prologue, 1.1-7, 2.6, 3.7, 4.3, Epilogue |

| Concept | Comment | Section |
|---------|---------|---------|
| Leadership (cont) - Instrumental leadership | The focus lies on the leader's empirical knowledge. The leader's actions are rationally chosen from a repertoire of learned behaviors and rules. | 1.1 |
| - Dynamic leadership | The focus lies on the leader's experiences here and now. The leader's actions in the present situation are chosen intuitively from learned behavior, or spontaneously developed in the current situation. | 1.1, 1.6, 2.6, 6.8 |
| Leading | The process through which leadership is performed as part of an assignment or in a social context. | Prologue, 1.1, 1.3-7, 2.2, 2.5-7, 3.6, 5.3, 5.6, 6.8, Epilogue, App 3 |
| Matrix | Here: a way to explain different conditions, processes and events in a group. See also Group Analysis. | 3.5-6, 4.4-5 |

| Concept | Comment | Section |
|---|---|---|
| Mirror Neurons | Nerve cells in the cerebral cortex, activated when a person in thought and action imitates another person's behavior. | 3.1, 4.1-2 |
| Paradigm | A framework of basic assumptions and ways of thinking commonly accepted in the scientific community. | 2.1, 2.6 |
| Personal defense | Behaviors common to all humans and activated when one's self-esteem is threatened, often to avoid experiencing fear, anxiety and other discomforts. | 1.5 |
| *Phronesis* | A Greek word for *wisdom in action* relevant to practical things, requiring an ability to discern good and right conduct and also to encourage virtue in others. | 1.2, 2.2, 5.3, 6.1, 6.8 |

| Concept | Comment | Section |
|---------|---------|---------|
| Prevailing culture | The perceptions, values and behaviors commonly accepted in a specific part of society, such as a region, a country or an organization. | 1.1-3, 2.5, 3.3, 4.4 |
| Psychodynamic | The psychic forms underlying an individual's experience and actions. These forms are unconscious and can be understood in the light of earlier experience, self-concept and relations to events and others. | 3.4 |
| Psychosocial | The process of exchange in groups, organizations and other social contexts – between individuals and between the individual and the social context. | 3.4, 3.6, 4.2 |
| Reductionism | The idea that complex contexts and phenomena can be described and explained by a few simple and basic mechanisms. | 4.6 |

| Concept | Comment | Section |
|---|---|---|
| Self | The subjectively experienced own persona, separate from the surrounding object-world. Self-experience is both conscious and unconscious. See also Ego | Prologue, 3.1, 3.2, 4.3, Epilogue |
| Self-Concept | A generic term for one's own impressions and perceptions of one's self (Self and Ego). | 1.1, 3.1-2, 3.7, 4.3-4, 5.4-5 |
| Self-Esteem | A neutral and uncensored evaluation of one's self and self-concept. | Prologue, 1.4-6, 3.2-3, 3.7, 4.3, 4.5, 5.3-4, 5.7, 6.8, App3 |
| Social context(s) | A generic concept for different situations and events – settings in which various persons are involved, and in which the development depends on how the individuals relate to each other and interact. | 1.1, 1.6, 3.2, 4.1, 4.5, 5.2-5, 6.2-3 |

| Concept | Comment | Section |
|---------|---------|---------|
| Social Responsibility | An organization's responsibility for the impact of its decisions and activities on society and environment. | 1.6, 6.3, 6.5, 6.7 |
| Social system | A group of humans, in which there are dependencies between the participants and also in relation to agreements and regulations. | 1.1, 1.3-4, 3.6, 4.5-6, 5.1, 5.3-4 |
| Stakeholder | Individuals, groups and organizations depending on or having the capacity to influence a specific activity. | 6.3, 6.5, 6.7 |
| Structure (in a social context) | Relations in space and time and their historical background, which can be decisive for human interaction. Structure exists on an unconscious level and can be made conscious. | 3.2, 3.4-5, 4.4, 4.7, 5.1, 5.6, 6.1, 6.5, 6.7 |

| Concept | Comment | Section |
|---|---|---|
| Sustainable development | According to the 1987 Brundtland Report: development that "meets the needs of the present without compromising the ability of future generations to meet their own needs" | 2.1, 2.7, 6.5 |
| Synapse | The connection between two nerve cells, transmitting signals within the central nerve system. | 2.3, 4.2 |
| Team | A group of individuals with a task and being dependent upon each other when performing the task. | Prologue, 1.3-4, 1.6, 3.1, 3.3-4, 3.6-8, 6.8 |
| Trust | Trust between various parties is based on expectations being fulfilled. The parties allow each other to show vulnerability and can stand being in conflict. | 1.3-4. 1.6, 1.7, 3.5, 3.7, 4.4, 5.3-4, 5.6-7, 6.3, 6.7, App 3 |
| Wisdom in Action | See *Phronesis* | 1.2, 2.2, 5.3 |

# APPENDIX 2: REFERENCES

## Chapter 1: Leading Self

* Nora Bateson, Small Arcs of Larger Circles: framing through other patterns, 2017

* Magnus Lagnevik, Ledning och ledarskap i olika företags-former,
(*Leading and Leadership in different types of co-opertions*), 1989

* Lena Lid Andersson, Ledarskapande retorik (*The Rhetorics of Leadership*), 2009

* Manfred F R Kets de Vries, Paradoxes: Clinical Approaches to Management, 1980

* Henry Mintzberg, 'Developing Leaders? Developing Countries' , 2010

* F. Holmes Atwater, The Hemi-Sync® Process, The Monroe Institute, 2004

* Håkan Lagergren, Mänskligt Ledarskap (*Human Leadership*), Håkan Lagergren, 2003

* George Binney, Gerhard Wilke, Colin Williams Living Leadership: A Practical Guide for Ordinary Heroes, 2005

* Peter Stevrin, Tillitskrisen: Om tillit, misstro och kontroll i det framväxande informationssamhället (*The Trust Crisis: On trust, mistrust, and control in the emerging information society*), 1998

* Edward L Deci & Richard M. Ryan, Intrinsic Motivation and Self-Determination in Human Behavior, 1985

* Antony C Colijn, Engaging Leadership: A New Road Taken, 2009

* John Bowlby, The Making and Breaking of Affectional Bonds, 1979

* Will Schutz,The Human Element: Productivity, Self-Esteem and the Bottom Line, 1994

## Chapter 2: The Task

* David Atterborough, Planet Earth, BBC, 2007
* William E. Rees & Mathias Wackernagel, Our Ecological Footprint: Reducing Human Impact on the Earth, 1996
* UN Commission on Environment and Development, Our Common Future, 1987
* Pierre Teilhard de Chardin, The Phenomenon of Man, 1975
* Mats R Larsson with Mike Szimanski, Overcoming Overuse of Energy, 2009

## Chapter 3: The Team

* Lasse Berg, Dawn over the Kalahari: How Humans Became Human, 2011
* Richard Dawkins, The Selfish Gene, 1989
* Daniel N. Stern, The Interpersonal World of the Infant: A View from Psychoanalysis and Developmental Psychology, 2000
* Will Schutz,
  – FIRO: A Three-Dimensional Theory of Interpersonal Behavior, 1958
  – The Human Element: Productivity, Self-Esteem and the Bottom Line, 1994
* Robert Plutchik, Emotions in the practice of Psychotherapy, 2000
* Wilfred Bion, Experiences in Groups and Other Papers, 1961
* S H Foulkes, Group Analytic Psychotherapy: Methods and Principles, 1975
* James W Tamm & Ronald J Luyet, Radical Collaboration, 2004
* Susan Wheelan, Group Processes: A Developmental Perspective, 2005

## Chapter 4: Awareness

* Joachim Bauer, Warum ich fühle was du fühlst: Intuitive Kommunikation und das Geheimnis der Spiegelneurone, (*Why I feel like you feel: Intuitive Communication and the Secret behind the Mirror Neurons*), 2005
* Brian Lancaster, Approaches to Consciousness, 2004
* Rolf Ekman & Bengt Arnetz (red), Stress, (*Stress*), 2005
* Lars Olsson et al, Hjärnan, (*The Brain*), 2007
* Susan Blackmore, Consciousness: An Introduction, 2010
* Åsa Nilsonne, Mindfulness i hjärnan, (*Mindfulness in the Brain*), 2009, 2016
* Aaadu Ott, Låt hjärnan va' me' ...!, (*Let the Brain be around .....!*), 2010
* F. Holmes Atwater, The Hemi-Sync® Process, The Monroe Institute, 2004
* Pat de Maré, Perspectives in Group Psychotherapy – A Theoretical Background, 1972
* Pat de Maré, Piper & Thompson, Koinonia: From Hate through Dialogue to Culture in the Larger Group, 1991
* Karen A Franck & Teresa von Sommaruga Howard, Design through Dialogue – A Guide for Clients and Architects, 2010
* Rush W Dozier, Jr, Fear Itself: The Origin and Nature of the Powerful Emotion That Shapes Our Lives and Our World, **1998**
* Thomas Metzinger, The Ego Tunnel: The Science of the Mind and the Myth of the Self, 2009
* Margaret Donaldson, Human Minds: An Exploration, 1992
* Ken Wilber, The integral vision, 2007

## Chapter 5: Dialogue

* Steven Pinker, The Blank Slate, 2003
* Philip Ball, Critical Mass, 2004
* Martin Buber, I and Thou, 1970
* Stephen M. R. Covey, The Speed of Trust, 2006

* Geert Hofstede, Cultures and Organizations: Software of the Mind, 2010
* Jon Elster, Vetenskapliga förklaringar, (*Scientific Explanations*), 1990
* Will Schutz,
  – FIRO: A Three-Dimensional Theory of Interpersonal Behavior, 1958
  – Beyond FIRO-B: Three new theory-derived measures – Element B: Behavior, Element F: Feelings, Element S: Self, 1992
  – The Human Element: Productivity: Self-Esteem and the Bottom Line, 1994
* Claes Janssen,
  – Personlig dialektik, (*Perssonal Dialectics*), 1975
  – Förändringens fyra rum (*The Four Rooms of Change*), 1996
* Bertil Magnusson, Om konsten att ändra andra, (*On the art of changing others*), 1995
* Robert Fritz, The Path of Least Resistance for Managers, 1999
* Gregory Bateson, Mind and Nature: A Necessary Unit, 1979
* Manfred F R Kets de Vries, Paradoxes: Clinical Approaches to Management, 1980
* Herbert C. Kelman, Processes of Opinion Change, Public Opinion Quarterly, 1961

## Chapter 6: Phronesis

* Stéphane Hessel, Time for Outrage: Indignez-vouz!, 2011
* José Luis Ramírez, Skapande mening, (*Creating Meaning*), 1995
* Francis Crick, The Astonishing Hypothesis: The Scientific Search for the Soul, 1994
* ISO/TMB/WG SR, ISO 26000: Guidance on Social Responsibility, 2010
* Wilhelm Röpke, A Humane Economy: The Social Framework of the Free Market, 1957
* FCCC/CP/2015/L.9: Adoption of the Paris Agreement, 2015

## Epilogue

*   Michael Puett & Christine Gross-Loh, The Path:
    A New Way to Think About Everything, 2016
*   Max Tegmark, Our Mathematical Universe:
    My Quest for the Ultimate Nature of Reality, 2014

## APPENDIX 3: The FIRO Theory –
## by Dag Rudqvist (in my translation).

Will Schutz introduced the FIRO theory in the 1950's. It was the outcome of his research for the US navy. Those responsible wanted to understand how to create efficient management teams.

One staring point was how different organisms could be understood through their demarcations and through how they maintain inner balance and balance in relations to their surrounding. Unbalance causes driving forces and change processes.

Schutz saw those unbalances and energy processes take place in humans at an early stage when relating to others and when interacting with others in a group.

Another starting point was that different investigations of social organizations described humans relating to each other from three different aspects and independent of context. He postulated a theory, **FIRO** – *Fundamental Interpersonal Relations Orientation* – on how these aspects could be used to understand how forces and processes develop as people relate to each other.

Schutz introduced his presentation of the FIRO theory with 'People need people' (1966). He used this starting point to develop how we need other people. He states that we need each other in order to be together, to control our existence and to get solicitude and love.

These three needs frame the basis of the three dimensions in the FIRO theory. He pointed out that these dimensions should not be looked upon as distinct phases in a sequence, rather as three of each other independent dimensions, all having an impact upon our way of thinking, feeling and acting in different situations.

These needs are like biological needs in the sense that if they cannot be met we suffer. We can even get sick and die.

## How these dimensions have been expressed in different contexts

The values of Liberty, Equality and Fraternity (Liberté, Égalité, Fraternité) emerged with the French revolution in 1789. These values are also the basis for The UN Declaration of Human Rights from 1948, a document that expresses the three FIRO dimensions. Liberty signifies that everyone can and should have the freedom to think. This freedom represents control and competence as expressed by the second dimension. Equality signifies that everyone is important and should be endowed with equal dignity. This is about inclusion and significance as expressed in the first dimension. Fraternity or brotherhood signifies love and solicitude as expressed in the third dimension (in those days in a patriarchal culture).

The Christian bible has the words 'Faith, Hope and Love', also expressing the three dimensions –
Faith/Control, Hope/Inclusion, Love/Affection.

In the Indian culture, Bhagadvad-Gita postulates three conditions for life: Devotion, Knowledge, and Goodness. Devotion expresses commitment and willingness to go for something (Inclusion). Knowledge expresses that competence is required (Control). Goodness is an expression of caring and loving (Affection).

Thus, the three FIRO dimensions have been applied in different cultural contexts in order to express and understand conditions for humans relating to each other and for a good life. Below is a presentation of the three dimensions in the format in which they were described by Will Schutz up to 1982 in the second edition of his book *Profound Simplicity*.

## INCLUSION
**attention – contact – solidarity – affiliation – commitment**

The inclusion dimension describes interaction between people in terms of words such as include, invite, be together, belong to, commit oneself, make invisible, ignore and exclude.

The needs and behaviors express giving and receiving attention and contact. To get attention I need to be discernible for others. To receive contact I need to be of interest to others. In ordert to give attention and contact, I need to be interested in others.

The question of commitment and obligation is raised in the meeting with others. I need to decide how much I want to engage, if I want to belong to the group and if I want to be participant or observer (to be in or out).

The need in the inclusion dimension has more to do with getting attention and participating in important contexts than with controlling and influencing or having an emotional experience.

My behavior connected to the inclusion dimension is dependent upon how I think of and feel for my value as a human being. These assumptions can be genuinely unconscious and shape the basis of my self-esteem.

If I do not experience myself as valuable, significant and important, I might be afraid that people will ignore me, not pay attention to me or leave me outside. My behavior in inclusion can go to extremes. Either I become obtrusive to make people see me or I become timid and reserved in order to avoid the risk of being ignored.

When being timid I want to keep distance. I might feel self-sufficient in order to defend myself against the perception that I am so insignificant that not anyone pays attention to me or want to deal with me. I might think that others do not understand me and that I might as well stay on my own and take care of myself.

When being obtrusive, I behave in order to make others pay attention to me. I seek contact with others and want them to do the same. I do not want to be alone. A more subtle way of getting attention is to be very competent in order to gain power, or to be caring in order to be liked.

My deepest and most painful unconscious perception at low self-esteem is that people are completely uninterested in me because I am of no value, insignificant and unimportant. My behavior aims at avoiding the unpleasant feeling of being conscious of this perception.

When being *'relevantly social'* I am comfortable both
when being inside and outside. I can choose my level
of engagement and commitment in a relation – depending on how I feel and on the situation. I can make
a strong commitment in a group or refuse commitment. I have a sound self-esteem and experience myself
as valuable and significant and I can therefore experience also others as valuable and significant.


## CONTROL
### controlling – leading – influencing

The control dimension describes interaction between
people in terms of words such as influence, power,
competition, control, surveillance, understand, master,
cope, competence, responsibility and model.

The needs and behaviors express giving and receiving
control and influence.

The need to control stretches from wanting to control
others to not wanting to control at all, from wanting to
be controlled by others to not wanting to be controlled
at all. My aim is to get enough control of my own life.

Expressing either independence and protest or compliance and acceptance shows that I am avoiding having others control me.

If I strive for power and influence, I want to be a winning participant or be on the winning side.

The need in the control dimension has more to do with control of my life than with attention and compassion.

My behavior in the control dimension is different from the inclusion behavior in the sense that it does not need to be visible. My behavior in control depends on how I think and feel about my capability to understand and cope with the situation, on my capacity to think and act and on my competence as a human being. These assumptions can be genuinely unconscious and constitute my basis of self-trust and of my self-esteem.

If I do not experience that I understand and cope, my behavior in control can go to extremes. Either I abdicate from responsibility or I take power and dominate.

When abdicating, I abstain from responsibility and power. By subordinating myself, I don't need to take responsibility or make decisions and take the risk of being disclosed. I want others to help me out and relieve me from commitments. I never make a decision and I rather refer to someone else. I only do what people tell me to do.

When dominating, I strive for power and want to be in control. A subtile way could be to compete. I am afraid that others won't let themselves be influenced by me and instead dominate me. I have difficulties trusting others, since I mistrust their competence. I want to show that I am capable – a defense against distrust towards myself. I take on too much responsibility.

My deepest and most painful perception at low self-esteem is that I unconsciously experience that I cannot understand or cope with the situation. My behavior aims at avoiding the unpleasent feeling of being conscious of this perception.

When I am 'relevantly capable', I am at ease when I control as well as when I abstain from controlling, when I am being led as well as when I do not led at all – whatever is appropriate in the current situation. I have a sound self-esteem and experience myself as competent. I know that others trust my capacity to understand, arrive at a conclusion, make a decision and implement as well as I can trust others competence and ability to take responsibility.

# AFFECTION
**love – affection – emotional – friendship**

The affection dimension describes interaction between people in terms of words such as love, affection, human solicitude, emotional closeness, like/dislike, personal, malevolence and friendship.

The needs and behaviors express giving and receiving love and genuine solicitude. It has more to do with caring for another person rather than giving attention and dominate.

My behavior in the affection dimension depends on how I think and feel about my likability and lovability. Is it possible to like and love me? These assumptions can be genuinely unconscious and are based on my self-love and on my self-esteem.

If I do not experience myself as lovable – rather as a malevolent and repugnant person fearing to be rejected – my behavior in affection can go to extremes. Either I avoid all close emotional bonds or I try to be *'over-personal'* with everybody.

When avoiding close emotional bonds, I am an impersonal stereotype. I keep the relation on a superficial, distanced level and I am most comfortable when others do the same to me. Unconsciously, I experience love and affection as very painful, because I think that it won't last. Therefore I avoid close relations. I avoid closeness and engagement. I even avoid caring for tothers. My subtile behavior is to be superficially nice with everyone.

When being *'over-personal'*, I tend to be very intimate, complying and trustworthy with others and I want others to behave the same way to me. To be liked is essential in my striving to avoid being rejected or not loved. A subtile way is to be affectionately dedicated to friends and jealously penalize their attempts to establish other relations.

My deepest and most painful perception at low self-esteem is that I unconsciously experience that I am not lovable. My behavior aims at avoiding the unpleasant feelng of being conscious of this perception.

When I am *'relevantly personal'*, I can choose my openness and closeness in relating emotionally to others, depending on the other person and the situation. I am aware of my need for love and solicitude and I have a sound self-love. Others not liking me does not mean that I am unlikable. I experience myself as lovable. I can give and receive genuine solicitude, affection and love.

## From FIRO-B to Element B, F, and S

As Will Schutz developed his original FIRO-B to the self-assessment instruments Element B, F, and S, he chose to change the designation of the third dimension from **Affection** to **Openness**. One reason was the difficulties that he experienced people had to interpret affection as a behavior. With the motivation that openness is an essential behavior connected to affections he chose OPENNESS to designate AFFECTION. The description of the **the openness dimension** remains the same as the one above of the affection dimension.

## REFERENCES to Appendix 3

Will Schutz
- FIRO: A Three-Dimensional Theory of Interpersonal Behavior, 1958
- Profound Simplicity, 1979, 1982, 1988
- Beyond FIRO-B: Three new theory-derived measures – Element B: Behavior, Element F: Feelings, Element S: Self, 1992

A C Bhaktivedanta Swami Prabhada, BHAGADVAD-GITA, 1985

The Bible, Authorized King James Version, 2008